GOING B[...]

Inside the Bankruptcy Business

Stephen Aris

CORONET BOOKS
Hodder and Stoughton

Copyright © 1985 by Stephen Aris

First published in Great Britain in
1985 by André Deutsch Limited

Coronet edition 1986

Aris, Stephen

    Going bust: inside the bankruptcy business.
    1.   Bankruptcy
    I.   Title
    332.7′5   HG3761

    ISBN 0–340–39456–0

Printed and bound in Great Britain for Hodder and
Stoughton Paperbacks, a division of Hodder and
Stoughton Ltd,, Mill Road, Dunton Green, Sevenoaks,
Kent (Editorial Office: 47 Bedford Square, London WC1B
3DP) by Richard Clay, (The Chaucer Press) Ltd, Bungay,
Suffolk

To Ben, Dan and Luke
to whom, I hope, it may never happen

Contents

Foreword

THIS BOOK is about what happens when people and companies run out of money – a familiar yet surprisingly unexplored subject. There are innumerable studies of success by journalists, academics and entrepreneurs themselves in which the Businessman as Hero figures large. I myself, in a book published some years ago about Jewish business in Britain,* have made a small contribution to this literature. But for every success there are dozens of failures. Statistics going back to Victorian times show that the odds against any new venture succeeding are more than three to one against. And yet something like a conspiracy of silence surrounds the subject. As John Argenti, one of the very few writers to explore this area, comments in his book *Corporate Collapse*:† 'For too long managers and writers on management have shown the tourist the sparkling city centre . . . and carefully kept him away from the slums and shanty towns.'

It is only recently, with the Government's decision to implement part but not all of the monumental Cork Committee's report on the reform of insolvency law and practice, that the subject is beginning to attract the attention that it deserves.

One reason for this neglect is that failure is a depressing subject. This has not been a cheerful book to write. Another, more important, is that bankruptcy and insolvency are dauntingly technical. The law is abstruse, complex and well-nigh impenetrable to all but the experts, who often speak in a language no one else can understand. The Cork Report itself is not exactly bedtime reading.

I do not pretend to be an expert. I am not qualified nor have I attempted to offer a detailed analysis of why companies, or people for that matter, fail. Nor do I have specialised legal knowledge. For those who want that kind of information I would recommend the standard textbooks of which there are now a large number.

My method has been quite simple. Fired by a reporter's curiosity about what happens when people and companies go bust, I have approached a large number of people – bankers, accountants, lawyers and businessmen, both large and small, and asked them what they did and why they did it. My object was to explore a largely hidden world and to throw some light on how people behave when the cash runs out.

The book is divided into two sections: the first deals with personal bankruptcy, the second with corporate failure. My examples are all recent and all British; as law and practice varies so widely from country to country, an examination of what happens in, say, Europe or the United States, would need another book.

The opening chapter describes the workings of the bankruptcy machine as it operates in Britain today. But as this machine still rests very largely on the foundations laid down by the Victorians I have thought it useful to take a brief look in Chapter Two at how society tackled the problem of bankruptcy in years gone by; especially as many of the abuses and scandals that were such a feature of Victorian and earlier eras are still with us today. The stern face of bankruptcy has changed less than one might imagine.

I conclude the section dealing with personal bankruptcy with two contrasting chapters: the first, Chapter Three, examines, by means of a number of detailed, contemporary case histories, the plight of the little man. Here we see just how painful and humiliating the experience of bankruptcy can be for the ignorant, the unfortunate and the unlucky. In Chapter Four I tell the story of Willie Stern, the failed property developer, who went bust for a world record sum of £118 million and yet continued to live like the millionaire he once was.

The second section of the book dealing with corporate failure looks first at the private world of the receiver and the liquidator – those dread figures who administer the last rites to dying companies. Chapters Six and Seven describe in some detail how easy it is for unscrupulous characters on both sides of the fence to manipulate the laws to their own advantage, to loot insolvent companies and to defraud shareholders, creditors, customers and employees. And the book concludes with two chapters in which I describe two of the biggest company crashes of the recent recession: Stone-Platt, the giant textile machinery firm, and Laker Airways, both of which collapsed early in 1982. Both episodes raise important questions about the attitude of the banks and their behaviour in moments of crisis.

In gathering this material I have relied very heavily on the goodwill and expertise of a large number of very busy people without whose help this book could never have been written. David Perrin, now of Thames TV and formerly with the BBC's Checkpoint programme, was almost entirely responsible for Chapter Seven 'Change the Name the Game's the Same' and also provided essential material for Chapter Six, 'The Cowboys'. The work of the BBC's Checkpoint team which, in a series of brilliant, hard-hitting investigative programmes has opened up an area largely ignored by Fleet Street, has been invaluable. And I owe a debt of gratitude to the programme's producer, John Edwards, who allowed me to plunder the files. Ed Harriman of Granada TV, Andrew Jennings of BBC TV's Watchdog programme and Colin Simpson, a former colleague on *The Sunday Times*, also provided valuable help and advice. Anthony Sampson and his wife Sally encouraged me to begin. The chapter on 'The Dispossessed' owes much to the selfless help of John McQueen who single-handed has waged a remarkable campaign on behalf of the unfortunate bankrupt.

Without guidance through the legal maze from David Graham, QC and Eben Hamilton, QC I would have become hopelessly lost. I have made some sharp comments on the behaviour of some members of the insolvency profession but this has not deterred many of its leading members from spending many hours giving me private tutorials on some of their more arcane practices. They have been more than patient and helpful. My especial thanks to Lindsay Denney of Spicer and Pegler who has pursued, with admirable single-mindedness, the rogue members of his profession and kindly read and corrected the first

13
)

draft of the 'Cowboy' chapter. Friends too were generous with time and comments. Don Berry read the entire book in draft and Berry Ritchie ran an expert eye over the Laker chapter. Nearly all the book was written in my spare time while I was employed by *The Sunday Times* but I am grateful to the Editor, Andrew Neil, for time off to complete the task. My family have been puzzled – and sometimes faintly alarmed – at my interest in the subject. But their support throughout has been unstinting.

Stephen Aris
Greenwich, August 1984

Jews in Business, Cape, London 1970

†McGraw Hill, London 1976

1 *The Machine*

NOBODY GOES TO Carey Street these days. The old London Bankruptcy Court building was pulled down years ago and these days all major High Court bankruptcy cases are heard in Court 46 on the first floor of the Thomas More building, a modern, appropriately severe block tucked away to one side of the Victorian Royal Courts of Justice in the Strand. On benches in the corridor outside the bankrupts sit, chatting in low voices, waiting their turn to enter the double doors of the courtroom and face their inquisitors: the Registrar, the Official Receiver and sometimes, but not always, the creditors themselves.

Court 46 is a modern, sparsely furnished room. It has none of the sense of theatre of the older law courts. The atmosphere is brisk and matter of fact. The Registrar sits alone on his high bench, conducting the public examinations or hearing bankrupts' applications for discharge. The day I went it was the turn of Mr Registrar Hunt to preside – a kindly looking gentleman with half-moon spectacles. The day's work starts at eleven. When I arrived, a little late, the first case of the morning was under way. Solicitors and barristers were in attendance, as was the Official Receiver, but of the debtor himself there was no sign. Plainly it was the Case of the Absent Debtor. He had, it appeared, departed for Switzerland giving, as the Registrar put it, 'no sufficient cause for his absence'. The Receiver suggested issuing a warrant for his arrest but this was turned down: no point, the Registrar said, when the missing man was in Switzerland; and besides, he murmured, if the debtor heard that there was a warrant out he might stay in Switzerland and never come back. So the hearing was adjourned *sine die*. Next case, please.

A dark complexioned man in his early thirties wearing

sneakers and a red kapok skiing jacket over an open-necked shirt hurried down from the back of the court and climbed into the witness box. There were dark lines under his eyes and he looked nervous and short of sleep. 'Please hold the Koran in your right hand and say after me . . .'

He turned out to be an Iranian student who had come to England aged seventeen with an inheritance worth between £15,000 to £20,000 in 1967 and over the next twelve years he had, it appeared, gambled the lot away. I see no reason to add to his sorrows by naming him so let us call him Aziz. He had already been through the preliminaries and that morning had arrived at the most formal part of the proceedings: the public examination prior to his bankruptcy. This has been a feature of the process for just on a century and is deliberately designed, as one barrister I know puts it, 'to thump the debtor'. Up until now his shame had been concealed behind the privacy of closed doors but now Aziz had to stand up on oath in court before everyone and give a public account of himself. It is, understandably, an ordeal that most debtors dread.

Aziz stood impassively while the Official Receiver in this case, a thin, meticulous man with the manner of an under-paid clerk, recited the facts to the court. Unlike company receivers who are almost invariably professional accountants, the O.R., as he is known in the trade, is a civil servant, part of the Department of Trade and Industry. At key points in the narrative he would clear his throat with a little dry cough. Standing at Aziz's elbow so that he too could see the incriminating piece of paper from which he was reading, the O.R. told the court that at the time of his bankruptcy Aziz had liabilities of £2216, including a debt of £1250 to Access, the credit card company, and a further £960 of debts to – and here he paused for a fraction for dramatic effect – to three gaming clubs. The debtor's assets, the O.R. remarked dryly, amounted to £10 with the result that there was a deficiency of £2206.

But how had Aziz got into this mess? That was the question that Aziz was there that morning to answer. On his arrival in England the young Aziz started off well enough. He learnt English, took A levels in maths, economics and English and began to study for a business diploma and later, at a crammers in Holborn, for accountancy qualifications. But before long things started to go badly wrong. He invested his inheritance in a building company in Iran which was lost when the company was engulfed in the Iranian revolution. And so in an effort to make good the losses Aziz took to the tables. At first he was spectacularly successful, winning over £77,000 over two or three years. And Aziz lived well: expensive clothes, hired cars and meals in smart restaurants.

'You were, were you not,' the O.R. asked in his precise way, 'extravagant in your standard of living?'

'Yes,' Aziz replied quietly.

But the money did not all go on high living, Aziz explained. 'I would win a lot but then I would lose a lot and at the end of five months I would be virtually penniless. So I would borrow from friends and try again and so the whole process would start all over again,' he said sadly. In January 1981 his luck finally ran out, the money from friends and family dried up and with no job and no resources Aziz fell back on social security. 'I'm living on supplementary benefits, I'm sorry to say.' The Registrar listened to this story with the air of a man who had heard it all often before. 'I'm afraid this is not a case where I can grant an automatic discharge,' he said. 'But you can of course apply at any time.' Of Aziz's friends, relatives and creditors there had been no sign. The only people in the court, apart from myself, were the debtor, the judge, three court officials and a bored news agency reporter. The hearing had lasted barely three-quarters of an hour and after it had finished Aziz wandered out into the late autumn sunshine. When I last saw him he was standing, still in a daze, peering at an official piece of paper in his hand.

However isolated Aziz might have felt he is not alone; the statistics, published each year by Dun and Bradstreet, show that bankruptcy is rising fast. According to Dun and Bradstreet the number of people going bankrupt between 1982 and 1983 rose by 25 per cent. And in the following year, with 8035 cases, it rose again by another 17·8 per cent, surpassing the all-time record set in 1976, the aftermath of the consumer boom three years before.

The official figures are not very revealing. They show, as one might expect, that the main victims are small businessmen: builders, restaurant and garage owners, taxi drivers and grocers. But for details of individual cases one must search the pages of the *London Gazette*, that austere and rather melancholy Government publication (annual subscription £229.50) that appears three times a week and which records, among other things, all company and personal failures. It is much read by accountants and bank managers. A page, taken at random in November 1983, reveals that the casualties come from all walks of life: carpenters and company directors, legal executives and shop fitters, fish-and-chip merchants and marketing men. There was the landlord of The Sow and Pigs of West Bromwich and the owner of John's Fruit and Veg of South Shields. There were plenty of greengrocers and butchers and even a former naval rating.

Just what combination of misfortune, bad judgement and incompetence brought these people into the Bankruptcy Court is not recorded. For that kind of information one has to go back almost a hundred years when bankruptcy statistics were taken much more seriously than they are now. In 1892, the year before the near-collapse of Baring Brothers, one of the City's grandest merchant banks, the then Inspector General of the newly established Government insolvency service analysed the causes of the year's failures, one of the worst on record. He concluded that although 'spectacular and often fraudulent adventures' were responsible for about a fifth, by far the largest number of failures, some 56 per cent, were caused by 'traders who have created, inherited, or otherwise succeeded to a legitimate and profitable business but who, owing to inexperience or in their haste to increase profits, are tempted into too rapid extensions or speculative ventures or fields of enterprise of which they have no previous experience frequently resorting to the use of accommodation bills.' In other words they financed their businesses on borrowed money and were quite unable to repay.

Though there are no current figures on the causes of bankruptcy to back this up, my own impression from talking to dozens of bankrupts, and that of the professionals, is that the picture today is very similar, in that dishonesty or extravagance is a factor in a comparatively small number of cases. The prodigal pools winner or the feckless football star may capture the headlines but most bankrupts, so the experts say, are little people who have been overwhelmed by circumstances beyond their control.

What has changed since the nineteenth century – and changed drastically – is the availability of credit. In Victorian times very few people lived on credit. 'It was a terrible job to get it,' said John Clementson who is London's senior Official Receiver and has been in the business since 1949. 'Certainly my parents had nothing to do with credit. They paid for everything in cash. They lived on their wages and regarded hire purchase as something sent by the devil. But today, what with credit cards and the like, people live quite differently: you are regarded as peculiar if you pay in cash.

'Even so,' Clementson says, 'the bulk of the bankrupts I have dealt with are basically honest. They would really like to pay their debts if they could. But they get into a mess, go into bankruptcy and then find they are trapped with no way out. I don't think the experience is quite as sudden or unexpected as they often pretend. Very often they can see it coming but they won't recognise it, even to themselves. And so they struggle on, say for a couple of years, until they are overwhelmed.'

Just as there are many roads to hell so there are many routes to bankruptcy. But once bust everybody, without exception, is subject to what Sir Kenneth Cork, the distinguished accountant and insolvency expert, has described as 'the draconian measures of bankruptcy'. Sir Kenneth speaks with some authority. He is not only a leading practitioner but he is the author of the monumental Cork Report which took five and a half years to write and runs to more than a quarter of a million words. Published in 1982 it is a document on a truly Victorian scale, appropriate to a subject so imbued with Victorian values. It is the most comprehensive attempt ever made to review the workings of bankruptcy legislation and to bring it into line with present-day conditions.

It is a remarkably hard-hitting report. 'The answers given by

British law today,' Sir Kenneth wrote, ' . . . do not seem to us or to many of those who gave evidence to us, to be in tune with modern needs, but responses to economic conditions and attitudes prevalent more than 100 years ago . . . The system for dealing with the problems created by insolvency has been tinkered with, patched and extended by false analogies, so that today it is replete with anomalies, inconsistencies and deficiencies . . . [The system] no longer accords with what the general public conceive to be the demands of fairness and justice to all in modern society.' Cork thinks that personal debtors, in particular, get a very poor deal. 'While it will always remain essential to punish the dishonest and reckless insolvent,' he says, 'it is also important to devise a system of law to deal compassionately with the honest though unfortunate debtor who is often no more than a bewildered, ill-informed and over-stretched consumer.' 'It is,' Sir Kenneth told the BBC Checkpoint programme in June 1982, 'utterly ridiculous for some little chap who only owes a little money to go through the rigours of bankruptcy.'

Later we shall see what happens to Sir Kenneth's 'little chaps'; what impact bankruptcy has had on their lives. But as this is a highly complex and little understood subject let us first take a brief look at the machine and the men and women who administer it.

The ground rules were laid down by Joseph Chamberlain almost exactly a hundred years ago and have astonishingly remained virtually unchanged ever since, giving rise to all kinds of problems and difficulties. And though at the time of writing the Government is introducing legislation to implement some of Cork's recommendations, the laws governing personal bankruptcy have remained virtually unchanged. In the autumn of 1983 one ingenious debtor from Lancashire sought to overturn the whole system by challenging the wording of the Bankruptcy Notice which has still retained its original Victorian language and which, he claimed, was invalid as it was calculated to 'puzzle, perplex and mislead'. The matter was debated by the High Court. And although the learned judges, on inspection, agreed that the document was indeed puzzling, perplexing and misleading, they had no alternative but to throw out the complaint as the whole machine would otherwise collapse; a prospect too dreadful to contemplate.

The main objection to the Act, however, is not its archaic language but the fact that it is quite out of date. When Joseph Chamberlain arrived at the Board of Trade after a triumphant career as an entrepreneur and reforming Mayor of Birmingham the legislators had been wrestling with the problems of bankruptcy for more than half a century: between 1820 and 1880 there had been, so one expert calculates, more than forty separate pieces of legislation. The basic problem had been to reconcile the competing claims of debtors and creditors; to find a system that was compassionate but just, hard but fair. Above all there was an urgent need to stamp out fraud. This was all the more pressing as the abuses that followed the 1869 Act which led to an uncontrolled scramble by unscrupulous creditors and their equally unscrupulous accomplices, the accountants, were nothing short of a national scandal.

'It would be impossible to exaggerate the abuses which arise, and which must necessarily arise, under a system which altogether depends on the honesty, intelligence and watchfulness of creditors from the carelessness with which proxies are given to unknown persons, enabling them to represent creditors not at one meeting and for one specific purpose but throughout the proceedings and for all purposes of the Act,' wrote Mansfield Parkyns, the Comptroller for Bankruptcy, in 1879. 'Beginning with the sale and barter of proxies a system of commissions and corruption prevails through every step of the proceedings under the Bankruptcy Act; solicitors are paid by the trustees they are able to appoint, either directly or (in liquidation) by the trustee improperly paying their costs without taxation, trustees being in turn paid by the auctioneers they employ and so on: the whole amount of these commissions necessarily coming in the end out of the pockets of the creditors . . . the present system leaves thousands of smaller cases to be scrambled for and in such a scramble the most unscrupulous are generally the most successful.'

Accountants and solicitors, appointing themselves, often by dubious means, as trustees and receivers, had a field day. And complaints about their excessive charges were legion. A shoemaker, for example, so small that his entire stock was valued at no more than £160, found that the receiver's bill, for no more than six days' work, came to £64 4s 6d. The receiver, said the Comptroller, belongs to 'that class of persons who are constantly on the look out for receiverships and trusteeships and is a bill of sale moneylender.' And even when the bankruptcies and liquidations were honestly conducted the costs were astronomical. In 1880 over 40 per cent of all assets realised from bankrupt estates were swallowed up in fees of one kind or another. The only people who seemed to profit were the small army of accountants and solicitors who lived off the proceeds of dead and dying companies. The fortunes of many of today's most distinguished accounting firms were laid during this period when companies were collapsing with distressing frequency. By 1867 two leading firms, Harding, Whinney and Gibbons (later Ernst and Whinney) and Coleman, Turquand, Youngs, had cornered the market in liquidations. The partners were so busy that they could devote no more than ten minutes a day to each case on their books.

These were boom years for bankruptcy: of all public companies founded between 1875 and 1883 more than one third collapsed, of which half failed within the first four years. But although these disasters provided rich pickings for the accountants, providing them in some years with up to 90 per cent of their income, their social standing was not high. Touting for business was common practice. The founder of one of today's big international firms wrote to a bankrupt: 'I am sorry to see your name in the *Gazette* and write to offer my services to prepare your balance sheet for the Court. You can rely on my doing anything for you in my power.'

Accountants were men to be shunned. 'Our social position was not enviable,' wrote Ernest Cooper, one of the founders of Cooper Brothers, looking back on the history of the firm which he joined in 1864. 'We may disregard the then current jibes, that if an accountant was required, he would be found at the bar of the nearest tavern to the Bankruptcy Court in Basinghall Street, and that an accountant was a man who had failed in everything else . . . but an accountant was regarded as associated with and dependent upon insolvency, and I well remember that to be seen talking to or having your office entered by an accountant was to be avoided, particularly in the stressful times of 1866.' In May 1880 the accountants, realising that all was not well, took steps to put their own house in order and set up the Institute of Chartered Accountants. But the abuses were so great it was clear that the stable could not be cleaned by the practitioners alone; legislation was required.

The result was the Bankruptcy Act of 1883. It was as much the product of the man as of the age. Joe Chamberlain was one of the outstanding characters of Gladstone's second administration: one of the very few self-made men to sit in the House of Commons, let alone on the front bench. He had made a fortune out of the manufacture of self-tapping screws and helped while still a very young man to build up the firm that became Guest, Keen and Nettlefold. He came from a stern Unitarian background and had been brought up to believe in the virtues of hard work, self-reliance and thrift. His father was a very frugal man and had a horror of debt. Shortly after his arrival in Birmingham to look after the family investment in what was then Nettlefold and Chamberlain, the teenage Joseph became a Sunday school teacher.

In almost every particular Chamberlain reflected the thinking of the new Liberal merchant class which had put the new administration into power. He, like them, was shocked by the scandals and was determined to raise, if he could, the moral standards of business life. In drafting his bill his first concern was to eradicate fraud. As he told the House during the Bill's second reading: 'This is not a matter which can be considered as a very exciting one or one which is greatly interesting. It does not lend itself to flights of eloquence; but it is a question which has a deep interest for great masses of our people, and especially for the great body of industrious tradesmen who see, with natural indignation, that under the present system, swindling is made so easy, so safe and so profitable . . . Every good bankruptcy law must have in view two main, and at the same time distinct, objects. First the honest administration of bankrupt estates, with a view to the fair and speedy distribution of the assets among the creditors whose property they were; secondly, following the idea that prevention was better than cure, to do something to improve the general tone of commercial morality, to promote honest trading, and to lessen the number of failures. In other words Parliament has to endeavour, as far as possible, to protect the salvage and also to diminish the number of wrecks.'

These are the principles on which the present law rests: for although the 1883 Act was amended in 1914, the basic provisions remained intact. As Chamberlain's biographer, J. L. Garvin, puts it: 'His bill struck at the very root of the evil by providing for vigorous enquiry and effective action.' The state moved in to hold the ring. A self-financing insolvency service, headed by an Inspector General in Bankruptcy, was set up under the Board of Trade. And sixty-seven Official Receivers set up shop in most big towns throughout the country. They were a new and strange breed of official, being both civil servants and officers of the court. Their powers were extremely wide. They could enforce compulsory liquidation of companies, summon meetings of creditors, administer the disposal of assets and initiate investigations for fraud.

Even so the Official Receiver was not all-powerful. When a company went into voluntary as opposed to compulsory liquidation, the private practitioners still handled the business. The Official Receiver stayed in the background as a kind of longstop and only moved in when things went wrong.

But if Chamberlain was hard on company fraudsters he was almost equally tough on the unfortunate but honest bankrupt. Exceptions were made for the mad and the illiterate but almost everybody else was caught in a net whose meshes were small enough to catch as many sprat as mackerel. Here too Chamberlain reflected both his own views and those of his constituents – the successful, hard-driving factory owners to whom unpaid debt was akin to highway robbery.

An elaborate system, still in force today, was designed to process the potential bankrupt. Any creditor who was owed more than £50 (a limit raised to £200 only a few years ago) could petition the court to put the debtor into bankruptcy. If the debt was not settled within three months he could, after paying a fee of £90, apply to the court for a bankruptcy notice, officially known as Form No 6 in Appendix 1 to the Bankruptcy Rules (SI 1952 No 2113). It is only the first in a blizzard of paper that descends on the head of the unhappy bankrupt.

The novelist, the late Colin MacInnes, who like many writers tended to pay less attention to the demands of the Inland Revenue than he should, has vividly described this stage of the proceedings: 'I was dying in bed, with tubes stuck into my arms, at the Hospital for Tropical Diseases, when a small man in a bowler crept into the ward and placed a grubby piece of paper on my belly. With faltering hands I raised the document to my feverish eyes: it was an Order in Bankruptcy.

'For some years prior to this nearly fatal illness, I had neglected to pay my Income Tax. Forms came, and the usual warning notices in black, then red, next letters peremptory or pleading, then admonitions from legal departments at ominous south coast addresses (the greater the danger, the further away the menacing office), till at last I was waylaid, in Camden Town, by a stranger who handed me a summons. I was to appear at the High Court to explain my neglect of civic duty. I failed to do so, and the Inland Revenue set the bankruptcy machine in motion ... From the moment you are made bankrupt, your Examiner takes over your existence and has powers over you greater than those of any man except a warder.'

From this point onwards the wheels of the bankruptcy machine begin to revolve with ever-increasing speed. To ignore a bankruptcy notice is to commit what the law calls 'an act of bankruptcy'. It is not the only way of going broke – what is quaintly called 'keeping house' (i.e. not being at home when the bailiffs call) is another – but it is by far the most common. And it leads inexorably to the issue of a receiving order and to the office of the Official Receiver.

At that moment the debtor crosses the bridge, and leaving polite society behind enters the shadowy world of bankruptcy.

It is often said of a drowning man that on the point of death his whole life passes before him. Much the same is true of bankruptcy. Most of the props that sustain lifestyle and identity are removed. All his possessions, save such essentials as beds, bedding and the tools of his trade up to the value of £50, pass into the custody of the Official Receiver to be held for the benefit of his creditors. All bank and savings accounts, insurance policies and other assets are either seized or frozen. The bankrupt can obtain no credit over £50 (the limit was £10 until 1977); with the result that telephone, gas and electricity are frequently cut off unless the bankrupt either puts down a cash deposit or agrees to the installation of a coin-in-the-slot meter. His business life is curtailed as he is forbidden, without the permission of the court, to act as a director of a company or to be concerned, either directly or indirectly, with the running of a business. And he is also prevented from playing any part in public life. The Act states that whilst an undischarged bankrupt he cannot serve as a Member of Parliament, a Justice of the Peace, a solicitor, a trustee in bankruptcy, a mayor, alderman, or councillor. Nor can he be a guardian of the poor, a member of a school or highway board, serve on a select vestry, or be a clergyman or an officer in the armed services. The final indignity, perhaps, is that any letters addressed to the bankrupt can be redirected to the Official Receiver.

The sole consolation for the loss of these liberties and rights is that under the protective cloak of the Official Receiver he has a shelter from the demands of his creditors. From now until the day of his discharge his affairs will be in the hands of either the Official Receiver or, if the estate is sufficiently large, of his trustee in bankruptcy who is obliged to pay any monies recovered, after the deduction of his fees, into a special Bank of England account.

The trustee in bankruptcy is a rather specialised animal who is usually called in by the creditors where the assets of the bankrupt estate exceed £4000. They are to the personal bankrupt what the liquidator is to the company. But they are not always as impartial as their title suggests: legally their responsibility is to the creditors and the creditors alone. And though they are appointed by the court, in practice standards vary widely. As Sir Kenneth Cork has pointed out: 'A good trustee will be human and try and help and advise the debtor but so many trustees are not experienced and they think their job is just to wind up the estate as though they are dealing with some impersonal creature that isn't human.' Usually they are solicitors or accountants who do the business as a sideline. But as the business can be lucrative – commissions vary from 10 to 20 per cent on assets realised or money brought in – quite a number of firms are beginning to specialise. Competition for business can be fierce. And whether the firm gets the job depends partly on its reputation and partly on how close it is to the creditors.

George Auger of the London accountants, Stoy Hayward, has the reputation of being one of the most successful in the business. A small, dapper man in his mid-forties he is as street-smart as a London sparrow. He has made his name in the bigger, splashier bankruptcies. He has an intimate knowledge of the financial affairs of such famous bankrupts as Willie Stern, the property tycoon whose career I shall describe in Chapter Four, George Best, the footballer, Lionel Bart, the composer, and Max Wall, the entertainer. But Auger, who started out after leaving Finchley County Grammar as a junior in the Official Receiver's office, seems happy to tackle almost any kind of job, from prising money out of an East End boxer to unravelling the tangles of Willie Stern's property empire. He is a kind of ferret in a dark suit with a sharp nose for where the money is to be found. And he takes proper pride in restoring the cash to its rightful owners – the creditors.

His work has given him a somewhat jaundiced view of the bankrupt and though he says he is sympathetic to the plight of the honest debtor most of his stories concern the hard cases. Over lunch one day he told me the story of one lady whose house he had taken as part of the bankruptcy proceedings. Some days later, after the house had been sold, the lady asked permission to go back and collect some children's toys – or so she said. But when the new owners took over they found that all the curtains and carpets had been slashed to ribbons. 'She must have come in with a Stanley knife when we weren't looking,' says Auger. But the business can have its funny side. Like many accountants Auger also acts as a company liquidator. He remembers one occasion he was winding up an undertaker's business. Some days after Auger had taken over as liquidator the managing director called to see him and pulling a handkerchief out of his pocket he asked for some cash. 'What for?' inquired Auger. 'Well,' said the managing director opening out the handkerchief to reveal a small, grey pile, 'this is the late Mr Brown and I need £50 for his casket.'

Although they have been around for more than a hundred years now few people have any clear idea of what Official Receivers actually do and how wide their powers are. Even financial journalists, who ought to know better, sometimes refer to the accountants who move in to wind up a company as the Official Receiver. The bankrupts themselves are often confused. 'The first question they usually ask is: "Are you going to take our bed?" ' said one young assistant from the Southampton office.

The confusion arises partly because the O.R.s themselves, like all good civil servants, deliberately adopt a very low profile, never seeking publicity. John Clementson, who as London's senior Official Receiver ranks only below the Inspector General himself, recalls an incident some years ago in Cardiff when a very awkward bankrupt, smarting from a well-nurtured sense of injustice, summoned the press to listen to his grievances. 'Even the London press came down,' Clementson remembers. The next day a highly coloured account of Mr Y's tangled affairs was blazoned all over the papers, much to the horror of the bureaucrats in London. The Inspector General himself was on the phone in a flash. What on earth have you been up to in Cardiff? he asked. 'We only just managed to wriggle out of that one,' says Clementson. The lady from the Department of Trade and Industry press office chipped in with an explanation. 'The insolvency service is not really used to talking to the press, you know. Of all our clients only the Patent Office is more nervous of the papers.'

What makes the office of the Official Receiver so forbidding is the all-pervading atmosphere of failure. The London headquarters are at Atlantic House, a faded thirties building overlooking Holborn Viaduct. From the windows of his office John Clementson has an aerial view of Smithfield Market. At lunchtime he can see well-fed advertising men trooping into one of the City's smarter and more expensive French restaurants. Even for a Government office it has a tatty, down-at-heel air. Underneath the notice 'Department of Employment' at the entrance somebody has scrawled: 'A joke, surely?' And in the anteroom, pages from the *London Gazette* are pinned to the walls listing forthcoming bankruptcy cases and creditors' meetings.

Clementson himself turned out to be less depressing. A solidly built Geordie in his early sixties he wears thick black spectacles and retains faint traces of his native Tyneside. His clothes were appropriately dark but his manner was that of a wise but rather harassed GP. 'I'm sorry to have kept you waiting,' he murmured, 'but we are terribly busy at the moment.' Clementson is near the top of his profession. He has the rank of an Under Secretary and earns £23,097 a year. He came up the hard way. He was one of the first to join the service after the war in 1947, starting as an assistant examiner in the provinces before climbing through the ranks. Like undertakers and taxmen he is faintly apologetic about what he does. 'It's not very glamorous, I suppose. But it's rather like being a dustman – somebody's got to do it. The problem is that when companies are being wound up we tend to get left with the cases that nobody else wants because there is no money in it.' In my travels around the insolvency service this was a complaint I was to hear many times. And it is plain that beneath the surface there is a good deal of friction between the under-paid, over-worked public servants of the O.R.'s office and the fast-moving, well-rewarded world of the private sector. 'When I first joined the service thirty-five years ago,' Charles Churcher, the Official Receiver in Southampton, told me, 'to be an O.R. was really something. The jobs were advertised in *The Times* and the pay was magnificent but today it's very different. Once the promising youngsters have got their basic training they are snapped up by the private firms and we are left to make do as best we can.' Churcher, who earns £18,000 a year, can't help looking enviously over his shoulder at the fat fees earned by the private accountants. 'The trouble is,' he says, 'that they just go down the list for those assets that are easily realisable and leave us with the rubbish.'

But whatever the disadvantages Britain's thirty-seven Official Receivers, backed by a staff of 1450, are obliged by law to soldier on. The service is expensive. The official statistics reveal that for every £1 realised in bankruptcy cases 57.3p went on administration expenses. But perhaps because of this it is one of the few branches of the Civil Service that manages, most years, to pay for itself – which is one reason why it was a candidate for privatisation. But the idea was quietly dropped after strong objections from the O.R.s themselves who argued that such a move would effectively put the clock back a hundred years or more.

To a man, the O.R.s protest that whatever the bankrupts may say, they are not hard-driving or unsympathetic. 'We are not oppressive people,' says Churcher. 'I don't go home to my wife and say, "I've had a lovely day. I've been horrid to everybody." ' But on balance, like the majority of the profession, Churcher's sympathies come down on the side of the creditor rather than the bankrupt. 'It's intolerable,' he says, 'that people who have worked very hard should be put in that situation. One of the functions of bankruptcy is to show people where they have gone wrong and to allow them to make a fresh start.' And Churcher argues that if they have to use a sledge-hammer to crack nuts that's not their fault. 'If you haven't got a nutcracker what else can you do?' he asks.

Churcher is a member of the old guard. But often the O.R.s are surprisingly frank about the shortcomings of the system which privately they regard as being unduly harsh. 'I remember,' says Clementson, 'when I was a very junior examiner in Bradford going into a house and finding it absolutely bare. There was just a woman and a couple of squalling kids. There was nothing in the house at all except for half a loaf on the table. It was really pitiful – a case for the social service people, not the bankruptcy courts . . . Undoubtedly the system needs reform,' he says. 'Basically we are working under a Victorian law which has not been changed for more than a century. It works all right for really big bankruptcies where large sums of money are involved and there are lots of aggrieved creditors. But it is not at all suitable for little people.'

For most of the time the O.R.s keep these thoughts to themselves. To the bankrupt they invariably appear stern and unbending, ever on the lookout for evidence of high living and loose accounting. One bankrupt I met was mortified to be questioned closely about why, when he owed his creditors thousands of pounds, he was still driving about in an expensive sports car. 'What's wrong with a bicycle?' the O.R. inquired. To march into a stranger's house and to take away all his personal possessions is not an easy job. But the O.R. and his staff, who are often surprisingly young, tend to hide their feelings behind a mask of professional detachment. 'I can't afford to get enormously involved,' says Southampton's Churcher, a large, rather caustic man who has the air of a harried schoolmaster whom life has somehow passed by. 'If I did I would go bonkers tomorrow.' These days Churcher deals with very few bankrupts himself. That job is left to the office junior, Michelle Newman, a slim, well-turned-out twenty-year-old with the regulation black skirt and white blouse, who came into the service straight from school and hopes, like many of her colleagues, to go into private practice once she has passed the accountancy exams. Michelle explained that she dealt with about one case a week on average. 'I try and let them know I'm coming, though sometimes they are not in when I call. That's what we call in the trade "keeping house". Some of them can be a bit awkward because they are often in a bit of a state. But they usually cool down after a while. I go in and look for the more obviously expensive things – televisions, jewellery and that sort of thing. And then I go and poke about in the outhouses.' I had been told by George Auger of his triumph when he discovered a shoe box full of pound notes buried in the garden – damp but intact – so I asked about that. 'Oh no,' said Michelle, 'I have never had to dig up the garden. We go a lot on what friends and relatives tell us. If the bankrupt has assets he has not told us about, very often they will know.' One of Michelle's colleagues said that banks were an essential source of information. 'Usually,' he said, 'bank mana-gers are quite willing to hand over details of a bankrupt's account because they know that if they refuse we can always get a court order.' Like her boss Michelle tries to keep her distance. 'If you get too involved, you get all caught up,' she explained. But wasn't this difficult for someone only just out of school? I inquired rather tactlessly. Michelle gave me a small, tight smile. 'You mature quickly in this job,' she said.

2 Pray Remember Poor Debtors

IF THERE IS little enough sympathy for bankrupts today, there was even less a hundred years ago and more. Society so disapproved of those who could not pay their debts that prison was the usual fate. However paltry the sum, debtors were treated little better – and sometimes worse – than common criminals. They were cheated, starved, and even tortured. And as they had no one to speak for them their complaints went largely unheard. It was not until the beginning of the nineteenth century that the public conscience began to stir and even then the pace of reform was agonisingly slow. The social upheaval created by the Industrial Revolution was so immense that the Victorians had little time or energy to worry about poor debtors. That anything was achieved at all was due at least initially to a handful of what we would now call do-gooders. The angry voice of Charles Dickens also had an effect.

In 1801 James Neild, a justice of the peace and treasurer of the newly founded Society for the Discharge and Relief of Persons Imprisoned for Small Debts, paid a visit to the Borough Compter, commonly known as The Clink and one of London's eight debtors' prisons. Neild was an experienced prison visitor. In order to compile a report for his society he had visited 146 prisons throughout the British Isles. Even so he was shocked by what he found at the Borough.

'Debtors,' he reported, 'have one small courtyard about 19 foot square. On the ground floor on the right hand, is the women's day and sleeping room, 24 feet by 9 feet and 6 inches. On the left is another, intended for men, 41 feet by 10; but the floor of this room being only of earth and mud and unfit to sleep on no use has been made of it for many years; so that men and

33

women associate promiscuously together in the women's apartments during the daytime.

'Above stairs,' Neild continued, 'are two rooms of the same size as the former; and these in 1801, were in good repair. All these rooms have fireplaces; but no coals are allowed; no bottles or saucepans to cook provisions; no mops, brooms or pails to keep the jail clean; no bedsteads, bedding nor even straw to lie upon. Hence the debtors are obliged every night to sleep in their clothes upon the dirty boards . . . Soap and towels are not afforded in to the prisoner; so that a man may, for the debt of one guinea remain in this wretched place forty days without once taking off his clothes or washing his hands and face.' Neild found the prisoners hungry as well as dirty. The basic ration was one twopenny loaf a day. 'This scanty provision,' he observed, 'without any nutritious liquor, only water, is not sufficient to support the cravings of nature; and the prisoner at his discharge may be fit for a hospital but he cannot be fit for labour.'

Neild was so upset by his discoveries that he wrote to the Lord Mayor of London, Sir Peter Perchard, to complain. Sir Peter did not reply.

It was hardly surprising. However indignant the philanthropists and prison reformers like Neild and his great predecessor, John Howard, may have been, Sir Peter, as representative of London's merchant community, could scarcely be expected to have much sympathy for people who were generally regarded as little more than parasites. When Balzac's M. Grandet declared that 'A bankrupt has committed the most dishonourable deed that a man can dishonour his name by being guilty of . . . [He] is a thief whom the law unfortunately takes under its protection,' he was expressing a widely held nineteenth-century view.

For the Victorians debt and bankruptcy were the ultimate catastrophe. It involved loss of possessions, self-respect and even liberty. Ruin is a theme that haunts many of the novels of the period. And many who failed preferred to end their own lives rather than face the stigma of bankruptcy. Trollope's Augustus Melmotte, the railway swindler and anti-hero of *The Way We Live Now*, chose to commit suicide by taking prussic acid in his house in Bruton Street rather than face the consequences; the shady City financier, Mr Dobbs Broughton of *The Last Chronicle of Barset*, suffered a similar fate when his schemes collapsed; and Charles Dickens's Mr Merdle in *Little Dorrit* met a particularly macabre end when he killed himself in a Turkish bath with a tortoiseshell penknife. Profits in Victorian Britain may have been large but retribution, when it came, was sudden and swift. To become a bankrupt was to become overnight a non-person.

It was an attitude that went back as far as the Romans. Under the Law of Twelve Tables creditors were, quite literally, given their pound of flesh: they could cut up the debtor's body into pieces and divide it up according to their individual claims.

The practice in seventeenth- and eighteenth-century England was only marginally less barbaric. In James I's time a crooked bankrupt could be 'set upon the pillory in some public place for the space of two hours and have one of his or her ears nailed to the pillory and cut off'. And in November 1761 one John Perrott was hanged at Smithfield for concealing part of his effects – the last occasion that anyone was hanged for fraudulent trading. Henceforth the fraudsters went to prison and the honest but bankrupt trader was merely driven out of polite society.

Since Elizabethan times the law had drawn a careful distinction between bankrupt traders and insolvent debtors. Recognising that traders could not live without credit, legal draftsmen drew up statutes which offered some measure of protection to the honest but unfortunate trader: creditors had full access to his goods and possessions but they could not lay hands on his body. Only if it could be proved that he had tried to salt away the assets in advance of his onrushing bankruptcy would the trader feel the full weight of the criminal law.

But if the prospect for bankrupt traders was poor that for insolvent debtors was even worse. They were treated as criminals irrespective of whether they had cheated their creditors – which meant in effect that there was one law for the poor and another for the rich. For centuries they had been completely at the mercy of their creditors who could send them to prison for the most trifling of sums. And there they remained until the money was repaid. When the Fleet prison was finally closed down in 1844 after more than six hundred years, off and on, as a debtors' prison, it was discovered that two prisoners had been there for more than thirty years. Once ensnared in the net woven by their creditors it was, as Dickens noted in *Little Dorrit*, his brilliant, savage indictment of the system, extraordinarily difficult to escape.

Dickens had an intimate knowledge of his subject. While still a child, his father, John Dickens, was committed for debt to the Marshalsea. During the day the twelve-year-old Dickens toiled at the blacking factory and after work he would cross the river to spend his evenings with his family in the Marshalsea. And when forty years later he came to write *Little Dorrit*, his portrait of William Dorrit, 'The Father of the Marshalsea', was largely based on his own father.

Of Mr Dorrit's plight Dickens wrote: 'The affairs of this debtor were perplexed by a partnership of which he knew no more than he had invested money in it; by legal matters of assignments and settlements, conveyance here, suspicion of unlawful preference of creditors in this direction and of mysterious spiriting away of property in that; and as nobody on the face of this earth could be more incapable of explaining any single item in the heap of confusion than the debtor himself, nothing comprehensible could be made of his case. To question him in detail and endeavour to reconcile his answers; to closet him with accountants and sharp practitioners learned in the wiles of insolvency and bankruptcy, was only to put the case out of compound interest and incomprehensibility ... "Out?" said the turnkey. "He'll never get out unless his creditors take him by the shoulders and shove him out." '

For the most part debtors like Mr Dorrit were little people. In 1801 the redoubtable James Neild, analysing the published figures, found that four-fifths of all those imprisoned for debt owed under £20. 'The extension of the law of arrests to simple contract debts,' Neild wrote, 'was an innovation on the ancient laws of the land; and yet, for the security of creditors in a commercial country it is invariably admitted as necessary. Principally, however, it affects the inferior class, the most helpless and numerous by continuance of imprisonment for want of bail; and stands in need of legislative correction.' Professional men, clergymen, traders whose business was too small for them to benefit from the protection of the bankruptcy laws, the foolish, the imprudent and the plain unlucky – all found themselves in the debtors' prison.

In August 1858 the Governor of Bedford prison, Robert Evan Evans, a humane and far-sighted man, reported: 'During the past week we have had a great accession to our numbers. Nine females have been committed at the suit of packmen ... It is really lamentable to see so many girls hurled into prison at the instance of these men.' Most of these girls, he added, had had goods which they had not ordered dumped on them and had been assured that no money was wanted at that stage. In other words the girls were victims of what is now known as 'inertia selling'.

The debtors themselves could, understandably, see little point in their confinement. And throughout the eighteenth century they frequently petitioned the House of Commons to redress their grievances. In 1728 the *House of Commons Journal* took note of a petition from debtors in Gloucester Castle who were, they said, pleading not only for themselves but for 'many thousands of prisoners confined in several gaols of this kingdom'. The *Journal* reported that 'through misfortune they were utterly incapable of paying their debts and have offered their all to satisfy their creditors who will not accept the same; so that they conceive their imprisonment is no advantage to their creditors, yet is a grave loss to the nation in general, the which by this prison is, with moderation, computed at £1000 per annum'. The debtors promised to deliver up everything they had to their creditors and asked to be released. But their pleas went unheeded.

The law was thoroughly unsatisfactory, both from the debtors' and the creditors' point of view. Unparalleled strength in one area was offset by extraordinary weakness in another. A creditor had, as a judgement in 1792 put it with chilling clarity, 'a right to the body of his debtor every hour till the debt was paid'. But once the debtor had been sent to prison, the creditor had no further redress. There was no mechanism beyond the threat of imprisonment for forcing the debtor to repay. So if he chose, the debtor could, from the security of the prison, defy his creditors and hold sheriffs, bailiffs and the like at bay for as long as he liked.

This was one of the first lessons Mr Dorrit learned on his arrival at the Marshalsea. 'We are quiet here,' a doctor told him. 'We don't get badgered here; there is no knocker here, sir, to be hammered at by creditors and bring a man's heart into his mouth. Nobody comes here to ask if a man's at home and to say that he'll stand at the doormat till he is. Nobody writes threatening letters about money to this place. It's freedom, sir. It's freedom.'

As the law stood it was only after the debtor was released from prison that he was required to repay his debts. Understand-ably some debtors took advantage of this provision: they often preferred to spend what money they had on living it up inside the prison rather than take their chances in the cold, unforgiving world outside. Nicholas Nixon, the deputy warden of the Fleet, told a Parliamentary committee in 1819 of a woman who had been in the prison for thirty years for a debt of £400 yet chose to remain where she was rather than face her creditors. The committee was much intrigued. 'Have you seen frequent in-stances of persons who have taken the benefit of the act who afterwards have made a good and gentleman-like appearance?' they asked. 'I have known a gentleman discharged under the insolvent act who has been down the Fleet market the next day, with a groom behind him, on two horses worth from 150 guineas to 200 guineas,' Nixon replied.

'They live luxuriously sometimes in the prison?'

'Yes.'

'Taking wine?'

'Yes.'

'Sometimes you have known them send for ice to cool their wine?'

'I have.'

But these were the exceptions. And although the system was open to abuse, by the beginning of the nineteenth century the practice of sending debtors to prison was increasingly seen to be both unjust and inefficient. Neither the creditors nor the debtors seemed to benefit and it was society that paid the cost as numerous critics pointed out. As a Royal Commission appointed in 1840 to examine the workings of the bankruptcy laws said: 'The distinction made between the merchant and the humble trader, in allowing liberty to one and taking it away from the other, pending inquiry, on the presumption that one is honest, and the other fraudulent, is not warranted by any principle either of justice or expediency ... The Insolvent Law, after interrupting a man in his business, taking away all his property, imprisoning him until his place of business is occupied, and then turning him out destitute, a proclaimed insolvent, and unworthy of trust, nevertheless expects him at some future time to acquire property which he is to give up to his creditors. The practical result is that he makes no exertion beyond supplying his daily wants and frequently becomes a permanently degraded character; his family are brought up ill; hence society loses and the creditors do not gain.' The committee saw no reason why insolvent debtors should be treated any differently from the bankrupt trader.

From medieval times debtors made up a substantial proportion of the prison population. In 1709 Daniel Defoe put the number, very conservatively, at 5000, dividing the prisoners into three classes: first there were the very poor, about 2000 in all, who were 'fed by the basket', as it was called, and who eked out their miserable rations by begging at the prison gate. One feature of London's Fleet that everybody seems to remember, as it appears in almost every contemporary account, was an iron-barred grate set into the wall overlooking what was then Farringdon Street – now New Bridge Street. On the arch above were engraved the words: 'Remember poor debtors – having no allowance'. There the poorest prisoners with assets of less than £5 stood in turn throughout the day, imploring the passers-by for alms. At the Fleet this feature disappeared early in the nineteenth century after it had been condemned by a Parliamentary inquiry as 'degrading'. But in many county gaols up and down the country the practice continued until well into the 1850s. Defoe's second category, again numbering about 2000, were members of the gentry and clergy, down on their luck. Their plight was even worse as they were unable to beg for food. The remainder were tradesmen and others who had 'something to bear them up under prison charges'.

Throughout the eighteenth century and well into the nineteenth, debtors often went hungry. In 1814 a House of Commons committee inquiring into the state of the gaols in the City of London had harsh things to say about Newgate which was then severely over-crowded: the gaol contained 160 debtors and 326 criminals against a planned capacity of 110 and 317 respectively. 'The allowance of food to debtors,' the committee reported, 'is 14 ounces of bread a day and eight stone of meat in every week, divided amongst all; but this quantity never varies ... it forms a very precarious addition; and the whole allowance is barely sufficient, without the assistance of friends, to support life. The manner of distributing the bread, which is given on every alternate day, is liable to this objection, that the prisoner is tempted on the first day to eat the allowance which is meant also to support him on the second; and that a person brought to the prison immediately after the hour of distribution, receives nothing for 48 hours and may be six days without receiving any meat.

'To the debtors, no coals or candles, no mops or pails are given. The Masters' side prisoners provide themselves with these necessaries; and those on the Commons side are able to procure them by subscription and garnish, and by various charities and legacies.'

That the debtors had barely enough to live on was bad enough: even more shocking, the committee thought, was that they were preyed upon by the gaolers themselves. Each prisoner on arrival was required to pay a kind of entrance fee, known as garnish. 'It is a disgraceful and oppressive custom and ought not to be permitted to exist,' the committee said. 'It is [our] decided opinion ... that the mode of remuneration arising out of the fees paid to the prisoner and by emoluments arising out of fees made at the expense of those who are confined to his charge is the most objectionable means by which a salary is given to the keeper of the prison. His interests are thus set invariably against his duty; and his profits are made at the expense of those whom the law supposes to be penniless and whose property belongs not to themselves but to their creditors.' The prisoners themselves, being closer to the problem, were more cynical. As one Fleet debtor versified in 1746:

> *Welcome, welcome brother debtor*
> *To this poor but merry place*
> *Where no bayliff, dun or sheriff*
> *Dare to shew their frightful face*
> *But kind sir as you're a stranger*
> *Down your garnish you must lay*
> *Or your coat will be in danger*
> *You must either strip or pay.*

That the prisons should be self-financing and that prisoners should contribute to their own upkeep was not a new idea. It was the principle on which prisons were run throughout the eighteenth century. The flaw in the system was the complete absence of any form of control: the prisons were 'farmed' and the wardens and others recouped the cost by charging whatever the market would bear. And as they were in charge of every aspect of the prisoners' lives every item, from accommodation to food, carried its own price tag. From the moment the prisoner was committed he was faced with a long line of officials – from judge's clerk to tipstaff, from turnkey to warden – each with his hand outstretched. Quite frequently the fees to all these necessary people amounted to more than the original debt – a theme which runs right through the subject.

Because the system operated behind high walls and locked doors it continued largely unnoticed and unchecked. But there were occasions when the smell of scandal became too strong to be ignored. In 1728 the affairs of the Fleet were investigated by the House of Commons. The inquiry centred on the activities of three men, John Huggins, Thomas Bambridge and Dougal Cuthbert, who were in charge of the Fleet at the time.

Some years before Huggins had bought a life interest in the

office of the warden of the Fleet from Lord Clarendon for £5000 and had proceeded to run the prison on a very loose rein indeed. He later told the committee that he had allowed so many people to escape while he was warden that he had lost count, having kept no record.

But Huggins was growing old and tired and so he sub-let the Fleet to two younger and more vigorous men, Bambridge, who became acting warden and Cuthbert, his assistant. The post was already highly lucrative. The MPs calculated that in 1728 the profits amounted to £4632 18s 6d a year – a truly enormous sum in eighteenth-century money. A small percentage came from letting out of 'sponging houses' – some thirteen tenements opposite the Fleet where prisoners could stay as the warden's private tenants while the money lasted. But the bulk of the warden's income came from fees, sale of privileges and back-handers of various kinds. A debtors' prison was, curious as it may seem, an ideal place to observe the power of money at work. Poverty may have been the rule but money bought all kinds of exceptions.

Once installed, Bambridge lost no time in maximising the return on his investment. The prisoners were milked for what little they were worth – and more. There was, for example, the sad case of Mr Robert Castell. On being committed to the Fleet, Castell was sent first to one of Bambridge's sponging houses from which he escaped by obtaining, for a fee, the so-called Liberty of the Rules. Under this regulation, peculiar to the Fleet and the King's Bench prison, prisoners were allowed to wander during the day in a prescribed area which lay roughly between the prison and St Paul's. But Bambridge continued to press the unhappy Castell for yet more money. And when he eventually refused he was sent back to the sponging house where smallpox was now raging. Castell protested, fearing for his life. But Bambridge showed no mercy – with the inevitable result. Within days Castell was dead, 'unhappily leaving,' so the Parliamentary committee reported, 'all his affairs in the greatest confusion and a numerous family of small children in the utmost distress.'

Where money was not forthcoming Bambridge resorted to torture. The committee gave a vivid account of the sufferings of

Senhor Jacob Mendez Solas, a Portuguese debtor. Describing the dungeon in the Fleet it said: 'This place is a vault like those in which the dead are interred and wherein the bodies of persons dying in the said prison are usually deposited ... It has no chimney, nor fireplace, nor any light but what comes over the door or through a hole of about eight inches square. It is neither paved nor boarded and the rough bricks appear on both sides and top being neither wainscotted nor plastered. What adds to the dampness and stench of the place is its being built over the common shoar and adjoining to the sink and dunghill where all the nastiness of the prison is cast. In this miserable place the poor wretch was kept by the said Bambridge manacled and shackled for nearly two months. At length on receiving five guineas from Mr Kemp, a friend of Solas's, Bambridge released the prisoner: but though his chains were taken off his terror remained ... this committee themselves saw an instance of the deep impression his sufferings had made upon him; for on his surmising that Bambridge was to return again as warden of the Fleet, he fainted and the blood started out of his mouth and nose.'

The investigation caused a great stir at the time. The painter William Hogarth depicted the occasion with a portrait of one of Bambridge's victims showing the committee the instruments with which he had been tortured. The committee's conclusion was forthright. 'These evil practices of letting out prisoners, extorting exhorbitant fees, suffering escapes and exercising all sorts of inhumanity for gain may in great measure be imparted to the venality of the warden's office; for the warden who buys the privilege of punishing others, does consequently sell his forbearance at high rates and repair his own charge and loss at the wretched expense of the ease and quiet of the miserable objects of his custody.' The courts, however, took a different view. Huggins and Bambridge were later tried for murder but acquitted through lack of evidence.

By the early nineteenth century the regime in the Fleet had become a good deal more relaxed. Behind the twenty-foot walls, topped with iron spikes, the prisoners lived in an enclosed, self-contained world with their own elaborate rules, habits and customs. Safe from their creditors they passed the long days playing racquets and skittles in the courtyard. They became so expert that the butchers from nearby Smithfield came in to challenge them. The office of racquet master was much prized as, like most other posts in the prison, it was a source of profit. And thus the prisoners competed eagerly among themselves each Christmas for the right to hold it. In December 1841, three years before the Fleet was pulled down, one John Aldrige of 2 Coffee Gallery, seeking the support of his fellow prisoners, issued a printed election address:

> Ladies and Gentlemen,
> The time having arrived when in conformity with the established rules of the place in which we are present inmates, it is customary for such persons as are desirous of becoming elected as Masters of the Racquet Grounds to canvass your votes. I do myself the honour of addressing you to request a continuation of the support that on a former occasion presumed me the appointment. I hope I may say my past conduct has been such as to render any protestations for the future save it shall be the same unnecessary.

History does not record, however, whether he got the job.

Self-government was the rule. A special committee, with president and secretary and representatives from each of the galleries, supervised the daily life of the prison: it heard complaints, determined disputes, levied fines and arranged the cleaning and the lighting. Galleries were to be swept every morning and washed once a week. And fines for blasphemy, swearing, riot and drunkenness were imposed at the committee's discretion. But the system did not appear to work very well. There were frequent complaints of loose living and general disorder which the authorities were quite unable to control. The unfortunate Mr Nixon, the deputy governor, confessed to the Parliamentary committee that the prison was a haunt of prostitutes. 'I very believe,' he said sadly, 'that it is the largest bawdy house in London; and these girls often get into riots in the gallery and there are sometimes fights; I lock them out whenever

I can.' And when he was asked why he did not intervene more often, he replied frankly: 'For fear of getting my head broke . . . When people are drunk,' he explained, 'any person going to put them to rights, most likely would have his head broke; a drunken man does not care much whose head he breaks; and in the dead of night I could not open my gates to go in.'

Class distinctions were rigidly observed. The richer prisoners lived in the four-storey main block, known as the Masters' Side. On each floor there were long galleries running the length of the building with small, ill-furnished rooms leading off on each side. The rooms were allocated by an elaborate system known as 'chummage' – another source of profit. Each new arrival was given a room but if this was already occupied the existing tenant could buy his continued privacy by paying the newcomer to go away and hire another room elsewhere from prisoners lucky enough to have free space. Some, after the necessary backhander to the warden, earned a substantial income from the 'chummage' system.

The poorer prisoners who had sworn in court that they were worth no more than £5 had no such advantages. They lived in a wing known as the Commons Side and shared large, barrack-like rooms with a fireplace at one end and sleeping cabins along the walls. As they could not afford the pleasures of the prison taproom and coffee house on the first floor of the main block, they spent much of the day either sitting in their rooms or begging at 'the grate'.

The atmosphere was a curious mixture of gaiety and gloom which Dickens captured brilliantly in *Pickwick Papers*:

In the galleries themselves, and more especially on the stair-cases, there lingered a great number of people, who came there, some because their rooms were empty and lonesome, others because they were restless and uncomfortable, and not possessed of the secret of exactly knowing what to do with themselves. There were many classes of people here, from the labouring man in his fustian jacket, to the broken-down spendthrift in his shawl dressing-gown, most appropriately out at the elbows; but there was the same air about them all – a vagabondish who's afraid sort of bearing, which is wholly indescribable in words but which any man can understand in one moment if he wish, by setting foot in the nearest debtors' prison, and looking at the very first group of people he sees there, with the same interest as Mr Pickwick did.

'It strikes me, Sam,' said Mr Pickwick, leaning over the iron rail at the stairhead. 'It strikes me, Sam, that imprisonment for debt is scarcely any punishment at all.'

'Think not, sir?' inquired Mr Weller.

'You see how those fellows drink and smoke and roar,' replied Mr Pickwick. 'It's quite impossible that they can mind it much.'

'Ah, that's just the very thing, sir,' replied Sam. 'They don't mind it: it's a regular holiday to them – all porter and skittles. It's t'other vuns as gets done over, with this sort of thing: them down-hearted fellers as can't swig away at the bar, nor play at skittles neither; them as would pay up if they could and gets low by being boxed up.' Mr Pickwick returned to his room in thoughtful mood and fell to reckoning how much his room was worth to the warden. He came to the conclusion that it was equal in annual value to the freehold of a small street in the suburbs of London.

When Dickens published *Pickwick Papers* in 1836 the Fleet had only a few years of useful life remaining. It was closed in 1844 and sold to the City who two years later pulled it down. Dickens did much to dramatise the iniquities of the system but in fact the evil had already been recognised, even by those most closely involved. Lawyers, accountants and others 'learned in the wiles of insolvency and bankruptcy', as Dickens put it, joined in a chorus of condemnation. As one experienced witness, both a barrister and a commissioner in bankruptcy, told a committee of City worthies examining the workings of the law in 1827: 'The creditors get no valuable dividend; and in addition to the loss of their money they have to pay the expenses of suing and imprisoning their debtor. This is an unnatural, a monstrous and a national evil and arises directly from the absurd legal fiction of considering all debtors as criminals in the first instance, and of subjecting them to three months' imprisonment before an equitable distribution of their property is admitted.'

The attacks came from all quarters. To the moralists like Dickens it was the human misery inflicted that mattered; to practical City men it was the inefficiency and the cost. James Neild, the debtors' friend, calculated that in Middlesex alone it cost creditors £3 in legal costs for every £1 of debt. Even so, so great was the Victorian horror of debt that it was not until 1861 that Parliament finally agreed to give insolvent debtors the same protection that bankrupts had enjoyed for centuries. And eight years later, in 1869, imprisonment for debt was all but abolished. Only those who clearly had the money but still refused to pay still went to prison — a penalty that was to remain in force for another hundred years. Some of the most blatant injustices had been finally removed. But the stigma of bankruptcy remained. Debtors may no longer go to prison but their lot is still an unhappy one — as we shall now see.

3 *The Dispossessed*

BANKRUPTS ARE NOT the easiest people to interview, as I quickly discovered. Quite early on I had been warned of the problems. 'You will find that bankrupts are on the whole not humble people,' said one accountant with long experience in the insolvency game. 'They are very good at finding excuses to cover up their own mistakes and inadequacies and blaming other people for their problems,' said another. 'Don't be deceived by all the stories you will hear about it being somebody else's fault. In my experience 90 per cent of bankrupts fail because of their inability to run a business. It's all right in a calm sea. We can all swim in those conditions. But when the waves get rough as they have been for the past few years then you need to be a good swimmer to survive.'

That may be true. But there is another, darker side to the picture. The accountants and others who run the machine tend to assume that once a person cannot pay his or her debts there is no alternative but to set the machine in motion and apply the full rigour of the law. But what is left out of this reckoning is the human and economic cost – both of which can be horrendous. 'Make no mistake,' said a third specialist, 'bankruptcy, for whatever reason, is a disaster: the costs are astronomical.' Once the process has started everybody takes their cut: the Official Receiver, the trustee, the solicitor, the valuer, the estate agent and the auctioneer – not to mention the Department of Trade and Industry. If goods have to be forcibly seized which happens quite rarely then the bailiffs and the removal men have to be paid. There is even a hefty fee to put oneself into bankruptcy. Frequently the costs of administering the bankrupt estate – a process that often drags on for years – far exceed the debt.

Michael Riley is a British Rail engine driver who went broke for a £641 debt to a finance company despite owning a £30,000 house. He was put into bankruptcy by the finance company which forced him to sell his house despite his offer to pay off the debt in monthly instalments. Other creditors were sucked into the action and by the time the solicitors had finished his legal bill was over £8000. In early 1983 he told the BBC Checkpoint programme: 'I thought I was a strong man but, my word, this has certainly broken me. To think that one can lose everything I've worked for and saved for simply because of a £641 debt which I had got covered in the first place. The truth of the whole matter is that in the initial stages I wasn't bankrupt but by God I am now.' At this point in the interview Mr Riley broke down and had to continue the narrative later. 'Once the machinery had started it was just impossible to stop it. It just ran over me like a steamroller and the whole procedure's going to finish me.'

But on top of the financial penalties there is the emotional cost. The trauma of going bust is, I discovered, so great that even years later many well-qualified and well-educated people found it difficult to explain clearly and dispassionately what had happened and why. Some were clearly suffering from what Sir Kenneth Cork describes in his report as 'bankruptcy neurosis' – an affliction that paralyses the will and leads to a belief that troubles are insurmountable. Driven into bankruptcy for quite small sums, even though their assets at the time far exceeded their debts, many people I met were shattered by what had happened and were obviously quite incapable of picking up the pieces of their ruined lives. The common idea that bankrupts are invariably inadequate and often dishonest people who take refuge in the bankruptcy courts in order to avoid their creditors is in my experience a myth. In gathering material for this book I have talked or written to dozens of bankrupts: company directors, hotel keepers, restaurant owners, builders and solicitors. Most were more than willing to talk to me, though one or two insisted on anonymity. 'We have been through quite enough already without advertising our troubles,' said one West Country businessman who had concealed the crash of his company from his wife's parents, even though they were extremely wealthy and could, in theory, have helped him out. Often, welcoming a sympathetic ear, they talked at length and in detail. They dragged out formidable dossiers chronicling every step of the disaster. The complexities were frequently mind-boggling. I came to feel that it was easier to understand the accounts of ICI than the ins and outs of why, say, some small restaurant in Croydon had collapsed. The Official Receiver and the trustee made regular appearances in the narratives, cast as bogeymen. And there were other bit players such as estate agents and solicitors. The most frequent complaint was that it was next to impossible to obtain expert and impartial advice, especially from solicitors; and even when it could be had the cost was dreadful. Two former policemen from Kent wrote to say that when they went bust they could find only one solicitor in the entire county who knew anything about the subject and added that despite frequent letters the trustee was quite unable to tell them how much they still owed. Another bankrupt wrote: 'The trustee has had on average about £7000 off me since 1978 and he informs me that no interest accrues to me as a bankrupt. Nevertheless my debts increase at 4 per cent per annum.'

But gradually, through the fog, a theme emerged. A small number of people I spoke to were plainly crooks or something very close. They tended to believe they were under no obligation at all to pay such things as income tax, rates or VAT. And when the Inland Revenue or the Customs and Excise pushed them into bankruptcy they mounted long and highly ingenious legal actions in the hope that their creditors would lose patience and eventually go away. Meanwhile they hung on to their houses and other assets for dear life. But these folk are very much in the minority: I shall describe their stratagems later. All that need be said now is that it requires more determination and legal expertise than most people possess to keep the machine at bay.

Most of the people I met, however, struck me as honest, if incompetent. In telling their stories they almost always frankly admitted that they had been foolish and/or unlucky. But equally they stressed that they never intended to go bankrupt and said that they would have been more than willing to repay their creditors, given half a chance. And those who had chosen, either through ignorance or poor advice, to put themselves into bankruptcy invariably bitterly regretted it.

One North Country builder, Jim McQueen, gave me a vivid account of what happened the day he ran out of cash. He is a large, burly man with a thick, bushy beard and very dark, glossy hair. He suffers from a heart condition, brought on, he says, largely by his problems, and now lives in a caravan with his wife and family on the Isle of Skye. He had, he explained, just started on a small job, putting in some windows, when a gentleman in a rather grubby suit arrived on the site and asked:

'Are you James William McQueen? I'm representing the Sheriff of Lancashire.'

'He pulled out a piece of paper,' McQueen recalls, 'told me to empty my pockets and hand over my wallet. "If you move anything, you will go straight to jail," he said.' The Sheriff's officer had been called in by one of McQueen's creditors whom he owed £120. (This episode took place before the limit was raised to £200.) 'I pleaded with him to give me four hours to try and raise the money but he would have none of it,' said McQueen.

'I asked: "What can I do?"

' "Declare yourself bankrupt."

' "But I don't want to go bankrupt."

' "You have no option."

'I was at my wit's end. I didn't know what to do,' McQueen recalls. 'The only thing I could think of was to go and see somebody I knew in the town whom I knew had gone bankrupt, but I found him and his wife in such an appalling condition that it was obvious I could expect no help there. I was advised to borrow £10 and to declare myself bankrupt. So I borrowed the money from my sister and did what I was told. Looking back I found it totally amazing. I was twenty four at the time and completely naive: I believed implicitly what I was told by professional people.

'Everything I had was taken. My main asset was my home – a modest, terraced house, three-storey, kitchen, bathroom and workshop. It was no great shakes but I guess it was the best house in the terrace. It was sold for £1200 – £400 under its market value. The first person who came to see it snapped it up the very first day it was on the market. We had a six-week-old baby but they gave us six weeks to leave the house.

'At the time I had trade debts of £500 and there was a £600 mortgage on the house. So I was expecting something back. But by the time I got out of it seven years later, what with fees and legal costs, the £500 had jumped to £2000. At no time did I ever have any personal debts.'

Eventually all the creditors were paid in full but those seven years had left a bitter taste. 'I came to feel that the whole of society was against me,' McQueen says. 'You must pay a price for owing money. And in this sense bankruptcy is as much symbolic as real. What angers me is the indiscriminate nature of it all . . . Everybody is branded with the same iron. Honesty does not come into it. I was once quite a successful businessman with a fair-sized business employing dozens of people. But once you have been a bankrupt you are over the fence. You are thrown out. You are isolated. My lawyer advised me to leave town. But I refused: "What have I got to run from?" I said. And so then the punches got harder.'

I had met Jim McQueen through his brother, John, a secondary school teacher from Lancaster who lives in a small semi-detached on a newish housing estate on the edge of town, overlooking a bleak plain criss-crossed with electricity pylons. In the distance rise the peaks of the Lake District.

John McQueen is highly intelligent and well educated: he has a degree in philosophy from Lancaster University. He is also very determined. He comes from a large, very close family – another brother lives next door. He has never been bankrupt himself but he was so appalled by what had happened to brother Jim, for whom he had worked at one time, that in the spring of 1983 he wrote to every national newspaper announcing his intention to start an association for bankrupts. 'Gamblers and alcoholics have their own self-help organisations, so why not bankrupts?' he argued. The national papers were not very interested; only *The Times* published his letter. But the local papers and radio were much more responsive. And within a few weeks letters from bankrupts all over the country began to flood in. McQueen's dossier contains letters from a striking cross-section of the population. Some were incoherent, some incomprehensible and some were eloquent and moving. But all expressed in their various ways the feelings of outrage, helplessness and despair that bankruptcy inevitably engenders. Of the 350 letters McQueen has received there is one which is worth quoting at length, even though it is anonymous. It came from a former accountant called Kay and recites with great clarity and detail a not untypical story.

KAY'S STORY

'As an accountant I had in the past dealt with many liquidations, and bankruptcies, being employed in a practice which specialised in such matters, hearing often the cry of the debtor: "But I don't owe as much as that," to which my stock answer would be an unsympathetic: "I'm afraid your affairs are in such a mess that you don't realise how much you owe."

'In the early 1960s my husband, then an official with the National Coal Board, was found to be suffering from pneumoconiosis, and we jointly decided that he would be better away from the mines . . . We decided to sell our home, and invest our savings in a business for him.

'A small corner grocery shop was bought in 1963, and I gave up my profession to assist my husband. This business flourished, and by the time it was sold in 1968 my husband was the owner of three large self-service stores, and we again had a beautiful private residence. We worked hard for long hours spending little on ourselves, or on our lifestyle, but never again made the ratio of net profit realised in the corner shop which we ran between us without help.

'In the self-service stores shoplifting was rife, and even a large percentage of the staff regarded their chosen perks as a right. We several times caught staff clearing large orders through the check-outs, but only a few shillings being rung in! To prosecute either shoplifters or staff was a waste of time, we tried it, and the publicity wasn't good for business, so after that the few we caught were merely sacked or banned.

'By early 1969 cash flow was becoming increasingly difficult, and bank overdraft increasing, so in desperation one of my husband's businesses was sold at a knockdown price, but this afforded only temporary relief; by the end of 1969 I knew that the situation could not be saved. Our home had been on the market for six months, the two remaining businesses, worth £25,000 and £18,500 respectively, did not result in sales. Here it must be noted that all the business interests were in my husband's name only, although I did have the right to sign cheques; our home too was in my husband's name.

'In January 1970 after a miserable Christmas, we filed our own petition ... So began ten long years, my engagement ring was removed from my finger and the liquidator eventually sold it for 5 per cent of its value, our home was sold for only what was owing on the mortgage (despite the fact that a firm offer for our asking price was made on the same day as we filed), and the beautiful furnishings, most of which were bought before our business venture, were virtually given away at auction.

'Even at the time of filing I knew that when we sold, our assets more than covered our liabilities. I kept the books, and our liabilities were just under £14,000; imagine my horror when the proxy claims were totalled at just over £40,000. Only one creditor had claimed the correct amount. The Board of Trade officials did not appear to take notice of our ledgers, or our protests: they only had a job to do and the proxies were accepted. We lost everything, and were left with less than a pound between us, but I can honestly say that nothing was hidden away with relatives or friends, even though we had a married daughter we could have used.

'I returned to my profession immediately, and my husband found work in a factory. We managed to rent a hovel of a house, probably because no one else was desperate enough to take it, and furnished the tiny abode from second-hand shops, until two years later the house almost fell down around us, and in the emergency we were allocated a council house in a high rise block.

'At the hearing, at which the Official Receiver stated that our books were the best he had ever seen, no order was made against our future earnings. My husband wanted to move to another area after the hearing, but I insisted that as we had personally done nothing "wrong", we should not run away, but rebuild our lives in the same city. Due to the nature of the work I was given permission to own a car and operate a bank account, from which I made monthly, voluntary payments into our bankrupt estate.

'After being allocated the council flat, every penny we could spare was spent on furnishing and decorating to the standard we had previously been used to.

'By 1974 we had our home the way we liked it, so I started saving, this time for a new car, a Triumph 2000 being bought for cash (new) in 1975. By early 1976, with our home the way we wanted it, the new car, and a few hundred in our own names in a building society, we thought we had almost rebuilt our lives. How wrong we were!

'Out of the blue we received a letter from the Board of Trade asking us for an interview. At this interview we were told that bankrupts were not allowed to own anything, to which I pointed out that I had permission to own a car, and operate a bank account, but the answer was that the car should only be a "runabout", and that we did not have permission for a building society account. Furthermore they knew to the last penny what we had in our accounts without us having to tell them. Our home was again inspected and the furnishings revalued. The outcome of all this was that the money in the building society was taken, the bank account was left as it was, the car was also revalued, and we were given the opportunity to buy from the Official Receiver our own car and furnishings, paying by monthly instalments . . . but we were warned not to buy anything further, or accumulate any savings prior to our discharge, otherwise they too would be "snatched" again.'

Kay concluded her account by apologising for writing anonymously but said that the letter had been 'extremely painful' to write. 'I wish now that I had listened to my husband when he said he wanted to move to another area in the beginning, as we spent ten years which neither of us would wish to relive. Now we have rebuilt our lives in a totally new area, no one around us

55

knows of our past, apart from the bank, we keep our skeleton in the unopened cupboard, and we wish to keep it that way . . . our strength has been sapped.'

THE SOLICITOR'S STORY

Like Kay, Annett Asirwatham is a skilled professional, a solicitor. I met him on a blazing summer's day – the hottest of the year – and we talked in the kitchen of his fifth floor flat in a run-down council estate in a South London suburb where he has lived since going bankrupt in November 1977. As there is only one living room, he uses the kitchen as a study: there was a typewriter on the breakfast table and three thick files containing the story of his bankruptcy stood on a shelf among the teacups.

He is a small, energetic man of sixty who plainly has been a battler all his life. He is a Tamil, a member of a small but much persecuted minority in his native Sri Lanka. The very week I saw him the island's capital, Colombo, was in turmoil as rioters drove thousands of Tamils from their homes and shops, killing hundreds. Asirwatham started out as a civil servant but quickly became involved in trade union affairs and played a prominent part in what was then Ceylon's first political strike to demand independence from the British in 1947. But when independence was finally achieved he lost his civil service job and started a legal practice, specialising in civil liberties and human rights cases – an activity which again was to lead him into trouble. During the emergency of 1970 he was detained for four months without trial and when trouble flared again in 1971 high-placed friends in the Government warned him that it might be in his best interests if he left the country. 'Last time unfortunately we had to lock you up. This time you might not be so lucky: there might be an accident,' he was told. Asirwatham took the hint and left for England with his wife and children. 'I had an insatiable desire to practise law at its source,' he says.

He settled in the South London suburb of Wallington and in 1974 set up his own practice as a solicitor, specialising in divorce and immigration cases. The immigrants paid cash, but the fees for many of the divorce cases came out of legal aid. Asirwatham worked hard and the practice grew, but as he always operated on very tight margins it only needed a small upset to throw the business off track. Even at the best of times he was hard pressed to break even and reckons that he was on average about £500 short each month.

So when the crisis came in 1977 it was not exactly a surprise. Overnight his office rent was more than doubled – from £3000 to £7000 a year – at a time when he owed £3000 to the bank. To relieve the pressure a friend, in return for a favour, offered to guarantee the bank debt himself – which seemed fine until the two men quarrelled. The consequence was that the friend paid off the bank, transferred the debt to himself and began proceedings to recover it by putting Asirwatham into bankruptcy.

At the time, Asirwatham was undoubtedly insolvent – but not by very much. The shortfall between his assets and his debts was some £2000; less, if £1000 owed by the Law Society in unpaid and unrecovered legal aid fees was taken into account. But what made matters far worse, Asirwatham says, was the behaviour of his trustee in bankruptcy, a Croydon accountant called Neville Eckley. From the start the two men did not get on. On his appointment Eckley wrote asking Asirwatham to come and see him. 'He treated me very harshly, like a criminal,' Asirwatham recalls.

'Look here,' Asirwatham protested, 'you are dealing with a qualified solicitor.'

'No, I'm not,' Eckley replied. 'I'm dealing with a bankrupt.'

Asirwatham makes a number of complaints about Eckley. He says that it took him eighteen months to recover the £1000 owing from the Law Society; that he put Asirwatham's house straight on to the market at £18,000 and ignored Asirwatham's pleas to hold back as the market was rising. And it was only after a strong rearguard action that Asirwatham succeeded in putting the house in the hands of his own estate agent who sold it for £21,500. Even so the amount realised for the bankrupt estate was less than expected. After the building society and the bank had been paid off, some £5500 was left, but this sum was reduced to only £3500 after Eckley had deducted £2000 for his own fees.

On top of this Asirwatham's ledgers went missing in the upheaval. Normally some weeks after a bankruptcy the bankrupt is summoned before the court for his public examination. But as Asirwatham's business records were missing no examination could be held and Asirwatham found himself in limbo. He claimed that at the start of the proceedings he had quite properly handed over his ledgers with everything else to Eckley but the trustee denied all knowledge. Normally an aggrieved bankrupt who wishes to complain about his trustee can make his case before a committee of inspection to whom a trustee is legally answerable. But in this case, for reasons that remain unclear, no committee of inspection was appointed.

Asirwatham was so appalled at this that he took the matter up first with the Official Receiver, then with the Department of Trade and Industry; and on obtaining no satisfaction from either he finally went to the Ombudsman. In September 1981 the Ombudsman delivered his judgement. He criticised the DTI for its failure to ensure the appointment of a committee of inspection, and solved the mystery of the missing ledgers. They were found in the hands of a firm of storage agents, but how they had got there nobody was able to say. And when, after the Ombudsman's report, a committee of inspection was finally appointed, it cut Eckley's fees by 50 per cent.

But by this time Asirwatham had been bankrupt for nearly four years, deprived of his house, his self-esteem, and his livelihood. He reckons that his inability to practise his profession has cost him £50,000 in income over the years.

When in January 1983 Asirwatham finally obtained his discharge, it transpired that his final debts amounted to £12,428 while the costs came to £6856. At the hearing the Registrar said that he was sorry he had been kept in bankruptcy longer than necessary. But though he is no longer a bankrupt Asirwatham is still paying a heavy price. The Law Society has ruled that despite his discharge he is still barred from practising on his own account. And as he can find no firm willing to employ an ex-bankrupt, sixty-year-old Sri Lankan solicitor, he remains on social security.

In telling this story Asirwatham had remained firmly in

control. But when I asked him how he had lived and what effect the affair had had on his family his voice thickened and his eyes filled with tears. 'The family has held together, thank God. There is one advantage coming from an Eastern background. We have a great tradition of family solidarity and loyalty. But it has been very hard for my wife and children.

'My daughter was engaged to be married when I went bankrupt but she postponed her wedding. She has stayed unmarried for the past five years,' he said, sobbing. ' "I can't marry, Father," she said. "I must give all my earnings to you." '

THE HOTEL KEEPER'S STORY

George Eastlake used to be the owner of a handsome hotel in the north east, the Minto Lodge Hotel at Newbiggin-on-Sea, a pleasant seaside resort in Northumberland. It is a place with strong mining traditions – Eastlake himself is the son of a pitman and his hotel was originally the local headquarters of the National Coal Board. Most of his customers were ex-miners who took particular pleasure in drinking in what used to be the boss's old premises. George and Mary Eastlake were well known and popular in the town so when in July 1972 the hotel business crashed it created something of a stir. 'Everywhere we went we were stopped and told what a crying shame it was and how it should never have happened,' Eastlake says.

George and Mary Eastlake now live far away from Northumberland. They share a small council house in a village just outside Dunstable in Bedfordshire where George has found a job as the deputy director of the local leisure centre. He is a quiet, studious man with a study full of books: philosophy and Bible studies are his speciality. But although his bankruptcy is now more than ten years behind him he still remembers it as if it were yesterday.

'We decided to put ourselves in bankruptcy. We went to the Receiver's office in Newcastle – St Nicholas building, opposite the cathedral. He asked us: "Do you really want to go bankrupt? Well, OK. Here's a couple of quid to cover the cost." And he gave us some little pink forms. And so we went back to the hotel.

'In a sense the worst was over. At least we had made the decision. The real period of stress was the preceding couple of days: all the emotion had been spent on the Wednesday and the Thursday. By Friday, the day we actually went bust, we were just numb.

'When we got home we found two big policemen who asked us: "Is it true that these licensed premises have been shut?" We said yes, it was, and they told us to keep it shut and not sell any more drink. Half an hour later a man knocked on the door and said he had come to serve a writ from one of our creditors. I told him he was too late because I had just gone bankrupt. "Christ," he replied, "it's just not my lucky day. I've got five writs to serve and I've not landed a single one. Three people were out, the fourth turned out to be the wrong bloke and now you . . . just my luck." So we gave him a cup of tea and wished him better luck next time.'

The collapse caused something of a panic in Newbiggin-on-Sea. There was, for example, the bride-to-be whose wedding reception was booked for the Saturday. 'What the hell am I going to do now?' she wailed. But the authorities, so Eastlake found to his surprise, did their best to be helpful. 'After I got the receiving order I went to see the Official Receiver's examiner. He asked me lots of questions like: had I paid the staff? How much cash did I have in hand?' Eastlake told him: £423. '£23?' queried the examiner. 'No, £423.' 'I don't think I have heard you right,' the examiner persisted. 'I think you will be needing the money. You have got £23, OK?' Eastlake then told the examiner he was living in a caravan which he was buying on hire purchase. 'I don't know anything about it,' said the examiner. 'Maybe I'll find out that you are living in a caravan later, much later . . . Meanwhile go away and have a good rest. And by the way don't forget to put some of your furniture in your mother-in-law's room. You will probably need it later.' The Receiver too was sympathetic. He was reluctant to see Eastlake putting himself into bankruptcy. 'I shouldn't do it if I were you. Law's very harsh. Lifetime of misery.' He looked and sounded remarkably like Dickens's Mr Jingle in *Pickwick Papers*. But once started the machine rolled on.

The next step was the public examination. Here too the atmosphere was Dickensian. The court usher, an old, old man with snuff on his robes which had turned green with age stood at the entrance to the court intoning:

'Bankrupts to the right, divorcees to the left.' There were only half a dozen people in the room, Eastlake recalls. There was one other bankrupt, a woman who displayed her indifference to the whole proceedings by propping her feet on the bench in front, the recorder, the clerk to the court and the Eastlakes themselves, crammed into a tiny witness box. 'The hearing was a complete formality,' Eastlake says. 'Nobody asked any real questions and the outcome was a foregone conclusion.'

Eastlake later showed me a transcript of his public examination. From this it is quite clear his enterprise was doomed from the start. The hotel was never profitable enough to repay even the interest on the substantial amounts he had borrowed from banks and others. But it is equally clear that Eastlake himself was not entirely to blame. He had not rushed into the project blindfold, had consulted with the lenders throughout and had taken advice from accountants, solicitors and other professionals. His misfortune was that the loans were substantially increased at the very moment when trade was dramatically turning down. For this the banks were just as much at fault as Eastlake himself – a point which the Official Receiver himself stressed in the course of his cross-examination. 'With the benefit of hindsight,' he remarked, 'it seems to me to be a crazy way of going about it – to advance a large sum of money at minimum or frozen repayments, and then to encourage you to take on another large sum at a very high rate of interest. It would have been better to have done it in two stages, I would have thought; to see how it was developing, and then develop again.' Eastlake replied that that was exactly his point. But by this stage it was far too late for post mortems.

Eastlake went broke for £83,000. The secured creditors were eventually repaid in full but one of his backers received nothing at all and another recovered only 6p in the pound. For his part

Eastlake lost his home, his hotel, his position in the town and all but a pitiful handful of possessions. 'The whole thing is dreadful,' he says. 'You join the ranks of a ghostly society that wanders around with very few rights and privileges. And it depends entirely on the resilience of the person concerned as to whether he ever gets off his back again.'

THE FARMER'S SON'S STORY

The farmer's son is so resilient that he would much prefer that his real name is not revealed. 'Quite honestly if I told my trustee everything I was up to I would be faced with some very awkward questions,' he confessed. So let's call him Peter. He had written to me of the stigma of bankruptcy. 'I feel it is going to be with me for the rest of my days and being only in my mid-thirties that could be a long time. I was once well off with no worries about the future; now we can only live from day to day.'

So when I eventually got to see him the encounter proved to be something of a surprise. The house, set back off a classic English village green surrounded by handsome eighteenth-century houses whose stones glowed yellow in the sunshine of an early winter afternoon, was newish and large; the sort built by prosperous farmers for themselves and described by estate agents as 'desirable'. There were two cars in the drive, both comparatively new. The drinks cabinet in the living room was well stocked with several kinds of whisky. Peter himself was a large, friendly man, dressed casually in slacks and sweater, with piercing blue eyes. I sat on the sofa with his wife beside me while he told me the story of his bankruptcy.

He had left school at sixteen to join the family farm and fruit and vegetable wholesale business. But as the farm was running smoothly, Peter, anxious to make a mark of his own, decided to branch out into the truck rental business. For a couple of years all went well. But when the downturn came in 1980 Peter found himself dangerously exposed. The company was a partnership so he was not protected by limited liability. Furthermore to raise the initial capital he had given personal guarantees and pledged his house to the bank. This was to prove his downfall for, when he went broke in October 1980, these were called in and he became liable for every penny of the £200,000 then owing. His bank account was frozen, his insurance policies seized and his business closed down and padlocked. Peter now bitterly regrets the partnership. 'If it had been a limited company I could have walked away and nobody would have batted an eyelid. If you owe personal debts and live extravagantly then you ought to pay them, sure,' he said. 'But if you run a business and then get caught in a downturn that is no fault of your own that's different. Why should we be hammered into the ground? The trouble is that if you go to the wall you are branded as a criminal even though it's no fault of your own. We lived modestly and didn't fiddle anything. We were just ordinary people.'

The only thing that saved them from complete disaster was that his wife had some money of her own. Like Peter himself, she comes from a wealthy farming family. With this small cushion behind him Peter set out to haul himself from the pit into which he had fallen. And in so doing he has been obliged, he said, to behave in a somewhat devious manner.

A highly ingenious and expensive legal action has been launched to ward off the bank's claim on the house. Peter's wife has argued that her position as a wife entitles her to half the matrimonial home, thus the bank is entitled to only half the house, even though it is in her husband's name and pledged against his debts. The bank is understandably resisting, for if this argument succeeds it would blow a very large hole in the law relating to guarantees and security through which hundreds would rush to avoid the full strictures of bankruptcy.

On going bankrupt Peter tramped the district looking for work. He had to find something as he did not want to live on his wife's savings, which in turn prevented him from claiming social security. 'That's the first thing they asked you: "What's your wife got?" ' he said. But regular work proved hard to find. 'The moment they heard I was bankrupt, they didn't want to know,' he said. He worked for a short spell for a double glazing firm, which itself went bankrupt. Peter then decided to set up his own two-man cleaning company. 'It's ideal work for somebody in my position,' he said. 'No credit and cash on the nail.' The company operates with his wife's bank account and earns good money. Last year it made £18,000. Peter's own car was bought from a friend who could not keep up the hire purchase payments but to avoid awkward questions it remains in the friend's name. 'But what about the creditors?' I asked. 'Aren't they entitled to their share?' 'No,' Peter replied. 'Not the way the law stands at present: it's all or nothing. If it's a choice of looking after my wife and family or the creditors, to my mind there is no argument. Wife and children come first.'

Nobody emerges from these stories with their reputations entirely intact. All, in their various ways, had been foolish or imprudent: the solicitor had over-traded, the hotel-keeper and the farmer's son had over-borrowed and the railwayman had over-spent and then fallen foul of a determined finance company. But equally, as far as I could tell, none of those I interviewed deliberately set out to deceive or defraud. There is something very odd about public attitudes to bankrupts. There is plenty of sympathy for the divorced, the bereaved and the unemployed. But when the cash runs out people tend to turn their faces to the wall. Real injustice, the product of bad laws, bad administration and bureaucratic inefficiency and indifference, goes uncorrected. No one, apart from a handful of enlightened professionals, is prepared to speak up for bankrupts. Most politicians are not interested: there are no great questions of policy involved nor are there any votes in it. The legal process is too slow and too expensive to offer real relief – a complaint that goes back to Victorian times and beyond. Only the toughest and the most determined succeed in battling through and the struggle is invariably long, exhausting and expensive.

Some officials do their best to temper a harsh system with common humanity; others see their duty to extend no further than strictly to apply the letter of the law. Solicitors and accountants, those best qualified to offer impartial help and advice, do not appear in a good light. The trustee seems, in at least one case we have looked at, to have been both greedy and incompetent. Nor do the unsecured creditors seem to have profited much unless the motive was simply revenge. There are plenty of losers in the bankruptcy game but where are the winners? Discounting the supporting army of solicitors and accountants, the answer seems to be: nowhere.

4 *The Biggest Bankrupt in the World*

WILLIAM STERN, one-time property developer, multi-millionaire and now freelance consultant, stands in sharp contrast to the rather sad characters we have just met. At the height of his fortunes in the late sixties he was invariably described as Britain's biggest private residential landlord. As managing director of the Freshwater Group he controlled more than 20,000 flats in London alone: an empire which only the larger local authorities could match.

But even in adversity he attracts superlatives. His business crashed in 1974 when the property bubble suddenly burst. And when, four years later, he went bankrupt for the truly amazing sum of £118,690,524, he earned an unwanted place in the *Guinness Book of Records* as the world's biggest bankrupt. And because these debts were backed by nothing more than his personal guarantee Stern was liable for every penny.

The public was astounded: how could anybody go bankrupt for such an unbelievable sum? But the professionals were unimpressed. 'It is,' said the Official Receiver in a remark that he must surely now regret, 'just an ordinary bankruptcy with noughts on the end.'

Stern claims to have suffered from the stigma of bankruptcy just as keenly as anyone else. He complains bitterly, as others do, of the difficulty of picking up the pieces and living a normal life. He said to me: 'While a bankrupt you are a marked individual. Whoever you speak to says: "Come back and talk to me when you have got your discharge." And there the conversation ends.'

But size apart, Stern is far from being an ordinary bankrupt. For reasons I shall explain later, he continues to live in some style in a magnificent £400,000 house on the edge of Hampstead Heath. He has three cars, a Jaguar XJ 4.2, a newish Honda Accord and a T-registered Ford Cortina in which the chauffeur drives the children to their private school. In 1979, the year after his bankruptcy, he applied for planning permission to build a £15,000 games room. And when his eldest daughter Miriam was married in 1982 another £15,000 was spent on a reception in a marquee on the lawn, followed by a slap-up meal for several hundred guests at London's Café Royal. The house contains valuable paintings and his wife has furs and jewellery valued some years ago at £49,000.

Stern and his wife Shoshana, it need hardly be said, enjoy a lavish life-style. At his application for discharge in the spring of 1983 he testified that between 1971 and 1978 he and his wife spent £639,000 on themselves – an average of £97,000 a year. The bulk of this money – some £457,000 – had come from Stern's own company, Wilstar, in the form of loans to his wife. That the money was taken in loans rather than in salary was for tax reasons, Stern later explained. And even after he went bankrupt the annual outgoings, so the court was told, were of the order of £30,000.

The creditors, on the other hand, have received only a tiny fraction of the sums owing – under £1 million – of which nearly all has been generously provided by Stern's long-suffering family in the States. From his own resources, however, Stern had contributed by early 1983 no more than £26,650.

Over the years Stern has been a frequent visitor to the courts. The most recent occasion was in the early spring of 1983 when he appeared in Court No 17 at the Royal Courts of Justice in the Strand before Mr Justice Walton to apply for his discharge. It was a full-dress High Court affair. There were no fewer than three QCs on hand plus the full supporting cast of junior barristers, solicitors and clerks; and, for once, the press benches were full. Willie Stern could always be relied on to make good copy. The case looked set to last a full fortnight.

For the first couple of days the applicant himself sat at the back of the court, occasionally whispering to his solicitor. During the recesses he nervously paced the corridors and did his best to avoid the newspapermen. There was some consternation in the Stern camp one morning when an alert photographer managed to snatch a picture of him on arrival smoking a cigar.

As always Stern was immaculately dressed; the image of a successful businessman. His suit was a dark-grey pin-stripe set off by a stiff-collared white shirt and a red tie with white spots. The only clue to his continental origin was that he wore his dark hair parted in the centre, brushed back from a high widow's peak with flecks of grey at the temples and revealing a small bald patch at the crown. He had a small, carefully trimmed moustache and he fiddled constantly with a pair of gold-rimmed spectacles.

In the witness box Stern did not make a good impression. By tradition, bankrupts applying for their discharge are expected to be both humble and contrite. Stern was neither. His manner was one of studied, elaborate courtesy. The judge was always addressed as 'My Lord'. But under a testing cross-examination his answers were frequently long-winded, over-precise and far from straightforward. This plainly irritated the judge who in his summing up said of Willie Stern: 'One of his defects is that he is incredibly argumentative on points which cannot be argued at all.'

The family is Jewish and strictly orthodox. Stern observes the tenets of Jewish law to the letter: he attends synagogue several times a week and scrupulously observes the strict dietary laws. For this reason, he says, he rarely, if ever, eats out and even refuses cups of coffee when making his business calls. To those outside the family circle he often appears difficult and stand-offish. The property world is a small one, much given to socialising and entertaining. But Willie Stern played no part in all this. 'In comparison with the leaders of the industry,' he has said, 'I lived like a hermit.'

In 1979 there was a minor scandal when it emerged that he had been in the habit of giving quite valuable Christmas presents to officials of one of his main backers, the Crown Agents, who had lent him some £40 million on the strength of nothing more than his personal guarantee. In court he justified these gifts, which included such items as a £400 silver tea service, by arguing that they were a substitute for the entertainment which he would but could not offer. 'I am proud of my moral standards,' he said. 'I know my own motives. I know I was doing nothing wrong.'

He was in his time a brilliant businessman with an unmatched eye for detail and a capacity for finding loopholes in the law which was later to stand him in good stead. He comes from a well-to-do Hungarian family. His father ran an old-fashioned textile business. But when the Nazis invaded Hungary at the beginning of the war the family was interned until 1944 when the Sterns made their way to Switzerland and settled in Geneva where young Willie went to school. In 1953 the family left Switzerland for America. In New York Stern studied first at the City University from which he graduated with a Phi Beta Kappa and then at the Harvard Law School where he took a doctor's degree in jurisprudence.

In 1956, while still a law student, the twenty-year-old Stern married Soshana Stempel, the stepdaughter of another Jewish refugee, Osias Freshwater, who had left Danzig (now Gdansk) for Britain in 1938. It was to prove an all-important alliance, for in 1960 it took him to Britain and led him into property at a most propitious moment. His stepfather-in-law was already a very rich man. With a company whose asset value exceeded £100 million he lived in great style in a splendid house in West Heath Avenue, Hampstead, which boasted six bedrooms, three kitchens, seven toilets, an onyx circular staircase and a marble entrance hall complete with Doric colonnade. Five years after his arrival in England Willie Stern moved in next door and set up an almost equally grand establishment.

Throughout the fifties, quietly and largely unnoticed, Osias Freshwater had built up a sizeable property empire. It ranged, so *The Sunday Times* said in 1970, from down-at-heel cottages in Tring and Brighton to prestige blocks in Kensington. But the jewel in the crown was some 20,000 comparatively modest but much sought-after flats in the London area. At first sight these flats did not seem to be a very fruitful investment; they were heavily mortgaged and showed a low return. Nor were the prospects much improved by the new Labour Government's 1965 Rent Act, hailed as the 'Tenants' Magna Carta'. Its

intention was to protect the tenant against the rapacious
landlord by enforcing a 'fair rent' and many property developers
saw it as a deliberate attack on the private landlord.

But Willie Stern, who the year before had worked his way up
from being a humble office manager to become Freshwater's
managing director at the age of twenty-eight, was not discour-
aged. With his sharp legal eye he scanned the clauses of the Act
and spotted a loophole: far from penalising the landlord the law
could, he saw, be turned to his advantage.

The concept of the 'fair rent' was central to the Act. In theory
most tenants now had the right to resist a rent increase by
appealing to the Rent Officer. For sitting tenants the Act
provided a good deal of protection. But new tenants were more
vulnerable: as flats were hard to get, they were more open to
persuasion, especially if the rents were low. What Stern discovered was that if they could, quite legitimately, be persuaded by
the landlord to agree to the new asking rent, it was a comparatively simple matter to have the new rents officially adjudged as
'fair'. All that was needed was for both parties to make a formal
application to the Rent Officer. Freshwater also went out of
their way to cultivate good relations with the rent officers,
entertaining them to lunch and offering bottles of whisky and
sherry at Christmastime. Once the new level of rents had been
established they could be used, thanks to a little-noticed clause
in the Act allowing landlords to review all rents every three
years, as a base to jack up the rents all round. The happy result
was that the capital value of the building rose dramatically,
enabling the group to borrow more money for fresh acquisi-
tions. Only three months after the passage of the Act, Stern
wrote in the *Investor's Chronicle*: 'This provides the best
possible protection against the eroding effects of inflation and
makes good quality residential investments more worthwhile
than commercial or shop lettings ... The next few years will
provide a better opportunity to acquire sound, remunerative
investments than has been the case since the end of the Second
World War.'

Despite the optimism, Stern was restless. He had proved
himself to be an ambitious, resourceful and able businessman

but perhaps he resented playing second fiddle to his stepfather-in-law; perhaps there were arguments about the speed of the company's development and concern about the size of its borrowings as Stern capitalised on the benefits of the Rent Act. Certainly Stern was a young man with much still to prove while Osias was over seventy and had already made more money than he could conceivably use. Stern himself has talked about 'generational problems' and hints at a family quarrel. And it is worth noting that when troubles came later it was not Osias who came to the rescue. But whatever the reason the fact remains that in 1971 Stern branched out on his own, taking his share of the family company which by now included an insurance company, a fringe bank and a good deal of property much of which had been mortgaged to the Norwich Union and the Legal and General Insurance companies. The total package had a net worth of £14 million – not a bad reward for eleven years' work.

But what had gone before was to pale into insignificance in comparison with what was to come. After reorganising his interests under the umbrella of a holding company called Wilstar, Stern changed direction and embarked on a huge spending spree. He moved away from residential property and into banking, insurance and, above all, commercial development. In the course of three hectic years he increased the assets of the group from a modest £14 million to a hefty £218 million. But as the value of the assets rose so did the debts, until at the time of the crash they exceeded £200 million. Even more crushing was the burden of interest payments which eventually came to £25 million a year, a sum about three times greater than the company's income. Furthermore this mountain of debt rested on a very tiny base, as the company itself had a paid-up capital of just £1 million. What prevented the whole edifice from toppling over was the underlying value of the property itself which, as we shall now see, proved far from stable.

It was the events of December 13, 1973, Black Tuesday, when Bank Rate, as it was then called, was raised to a record 13 per cent, that dealt the Wilstar group the fatal blow, even though Stern did not recognise it at the time. 'Nobody of any experience was warning of a crash. And if I failed to foresee it I was in very good company,' he said later. But in fact the writing was on the wall: property prices began a slide which accelerated throughout the winter and into the spring. As they did so the great property multiplier went abruptly into reverse. All of a sudden what looked like a solid enterprise stood revealed as a house of cards. By early in the New Year Wilstar was seriously short of cash to pay the interest on outstanding loans. This, however, did not inhibit him from spending £23,250 on a handsome present for his wife, a 6.15 carat diamond ring which was revalued a year later at £43,000. But with the market collapsing all around him Stern was unable to sell property to meet the debts. In desperation he approached the Crown Agents for further loans. The Crown Agents were by now so deeply involved that they concluded that the only solution was to lend their way out of trouble. But relief was to be short-lived. By this time Stern was not the only property company in trouble. The Bank of England was engaged in a full-scale rescue operation. Initially the Bank encouraged the National Westminster to support Stern but after receiving a pessimistic report from the accountants, Peat, Marwick, Mitchell, the bank concluded that Stern was beyond rescue and on May 9, 1974, called in Cork Gully as receivers.

Stern had no magic formula. Like the rest of the operators in the heady years of the property boom of the early 70s he was relying on inflation to make him rich: as long as property prices continued to rise, so too would the capital value of the buildings, which could then be used as collateral for further loans for yet more expansion. The theory may sound absurdly simple but it is one that even highly intelligent people find difficult to grasp. As the judge hearing Stern's application for discharge remarked: 'A sound ship should not take on water. But surely if there was stormy water ahead it would have been prudent to shorten sail and batten down the hatches: that is a metaphor that occurs to any Englishman . . . Why should you,' the judge inquired, 'crowd on sail when stormy water lies ahead? That for the life of me I find difficult to understand.' Stern acknowledged that with the benefit of hindsight the judge had a point. But he replied:

'That the market should disappear overnight was something we could not foresee. It simply did not occur to us.'

The real mystery of the Stern affair is not why he behaved as he did but why otherwise sober and responsible banks came to lend him such huge sums of money on the basis of nothing more than his personal guarantee. It must have been perfectly plain to such lenders as Keyser Ullmann, the City merchant bank which ultimately had to be rescued by the Bank of England, and to the Crown Agents who suffered the humiliation of a full-scale judicial tribunal of inquiry, that even if Stern was as rich as Croesus, if the bubble burst he would be hard-pressed to find £100 million. And yet the money flowed. Even at the eleventh hour, in the spring of 1974 with Stern on the very brink of collapse, one of his main backers, the Crown Agents, was apparently quite happy to lend more. Indeed in the three months immediately before the crash the Crown Agents more than doubled the amounts on loan to Stern.

Part of the answer to this mystery was that everybody was prepared to take Willie Stern on trust. Astonishingly the Crown Agents, as the officials later confessed to the tribunal, did not bother to check the state of Stern's finances or to probe the companies themselves very deeply. The tribunal found that no one had made any serious effort to check Stern's claim that his companies had considerable assets, nor did anybody take any steps to withhold the cash until those checks had been made. As one official told the inquiry: 'I knew nothing about Stern's personal finances other than his ownership of shares in his companies. I made no personal enquiries about his personal guarantees other than his companies.' The Crown Agents were not alone in taking a somewhat cavalier attitude to Stern's guarantees. The former chief general manager of the Midland Bank went as far as to suggest that the point of a personal guarantee is not to render the borrower personally liable but is simply a token gesture to ensure that he remains committed to the business. If that really is the case then the gap between City and High Street banking would seem to be even wider than is commonly supposed.

If Stern had a secret it lay in his character and his approach.

The bankers found him infinitely reassuring. His manner was always sober, punctilious and correct. And his belief in himself was so absolute as to be infectious. He invariably gave the impression of being a very rich man. 'He must be a millionaire several times over,' ventured one Crown Agents official during a discussion about the wisdom of accepting Stern's guarantees. And yet when the crash came in May 1974 these same guarantees were revealed as being almost worthless. Far from being a multi-millionaire, Stern's own assets were later assessed at his bankruptcy hearing at no more than £4462 – a sum which included £500 in personal possessions. As Mr Justice Walton remarked in his summing up: 'The whole question of personal guarantees was, and I mean this in no pejorative sense, largely a confidence trick. In other words Stern was supposed to be a person of great wealth. A person of that nature does not normally have all his eggs in one basket. Unfortunately that was exactly what Mr Stern had.' Even more unfortunately, he might have added, the biggest eggs – the house in West Heath Avenue and its contents – were to be removed from the basket and placed beyond the reach of the creditors. Stern was about to demonstrate that for some people at least there is life after bankruptcy.

However desperate Stern's plight might have seemed it was by no means certain that he would actually go bankrupt. At this stage the creditors, with the exception of the First National Finance Corporation which was owed nearly £10 million, calculated that there was more to gain by saving Willie Stern than from ruining him – a view shared by the liquidator, Sir Kenneth Cork, and the Bank of England which put discreet pressure on First National to drop its bankruptcy action.

There was much work to be done. Stern's affairs were in such a tangle that only Stern himself knew enough to sort out the mess. It was therefore agreed that he should work for Cork Gully as a consultant, initially on £15,000 a year, later reduced to a nominal £1000 a year. His job was to help Sir Kenneth and a senior partner, Gerry Weiss, to dismantle his own empire. The plan, known as 'Cork's dam', envisaged an orderly sale. Instead of flooding the market with the entire portfolio, blocks were to be released in dribs and drabs. In return the creditors would hold back and not press their claims. As large parts of the Stern empire were tenanted blocks of flats, there were the inevitable bargains. Melbury Court in London's Kensington High Street, for example, valued on the books at £2.2 million, was knocked down to the tenants' association for £1.25 million. Likewise Bournemouth's Bath Hill Court, described as one of the finest properties on the South Coast, went for £875,000 as against a list price of £1.18 million. The purchaser, David Tannen, turned out to be a very distant relation – the son of Osias Freshwater's half cousin. But although 'Cork's dam' had the desired effect the sales realised only a small fraction of the debts.

Behind all the wheeling and dealing loomed the problem of the £457,000 that Stern's wife, Shoshana, had borrowed from the master company, Wilstar, to furnish the house. This money quite clearly belonged to the now insolvent company and Cork Gully's Gerry Weiss was pressing for it to be repaid. But how? The only asset the Sterns possessed that was sufficiently large was the house in West Heath Avenue. And so arose the awful possibility that Stern would lose not only his companies but his house as well. Similarly, if the creditors ever lost patience and decided to put Stern into bankruptcy the house would again be at risk. He would suffer the fate that has overtaken many much smaller men before him. Stern therefore sent urgent messages to his father in America and consulted his lawyers.

The bankruptcy laws, as we have already seen, are exceptionally severe. But there is one loophole through which many bankrupts have escaped. Section 42 of the Bankruptcy Act of 1914, essentially a tidied-up version of the 1883 Act, lays down that if assets are sold or transferred at least two years before a debtor's bankruptcy then the creditors have no claim unless it can be shown that the debtor was insolvent at the time. Even then if it can be proved that the transaction was done in good faith and at a proper price the deal will stand. It was a clause that was to cause much argument later when Stern's trustee in bankruptcy, the ubiquitous George Auger, challenged the legality of Stern's manoeuvres, but the matter was never brought to the test as the Stern family settled out of court for £200,000.

Usually it is the wife who benefits from Section 42 which is why this practice is often known as 'In the wife's name'. But in this case it was Stern's father, Edmund Stern, who came to the rescue by offering to buy the house and its contents and to hold it in trust for Stern's children. The plan, which was first mooted in the late autumn of 1974, less than six months after the crash, was that Edmund Stern would pay the market price for the house, then independently valued at £110,000, plus a further £69,000 for the contents and the wife's furs and jewellery. It was understood that part of the money would be used to help Mrs Stern pay off some of the Wilstar loan and that part could be used to sustain the Stern family in the manner of life to which they had grown accustomed. But there was no firm agreement as to what proportion should go to the creditors and what should be kept for the benefit of the Sterns themselves. That apparently was left to Willie Stern's own discretion.

In court under cross-examination Stern confirmed that what triggered the deal was the threat of his impending bankruptcy. 'When the possibility of my own bankruptcy and that of my wife's became clear,' he wrote to Cork Gully's Gerry Weiss in November 1974, 'a helping hand was promised and it is in this context that the idea of selling the house to my father was conceived.' When Weiss heard of this plan he was highly critical. He replied: 'This could not be a worse sale. You have taken away the possibility of waiting for a better time and have given the proceeds to your children.' But Stern was adamant. 'I should not spurn my family's generosity just to please my creditors,' he argued. At the back of his mind was the thought that the creditors could put him into bankruptcy at any moment and that if he delayed too long he could fall foul of Section 42's two-year rule. As things turned out he need not have worried. The creditors stayed their hands until the end of 1977 and it was not until May 30, 1978, after petitions had been filed by Keyser Ullmann and others, that Stern was formally adjudged bankrupt.

Five years later, in March 1983, Stern came to court again to apply for his discharge. For six long days Stern and his lawyers attempted to persuade the court that he had served his time and that the crushing burden of debt should now be lifted from his well-tailored shoulders. The case would have lasted even longer had not the family in New York, after much to-ing and fro-ing on the transatlantic telephone, sent a message that it was willing to hand over a further £500,000 to help pay the creditors and the lawyers whose fees had by then risen to £85,000.

Even so the judge was not altogether satisfied. 'I see no point in keeping Mr Stern as a bankrupt indefinitely,' he said. 'Whatever Mr Stern's faults – and they are many – he is an exceptionally able businessman if only he could keep to the right path. The transactions over the house do not redound wholly to his credit.' So, the judge continued, has Mr Stern learned the lessons of his bankruptcy? Is he prepared to conduct himself as a businessman of his ability and religious persuasion should? 'I regret to say that the moment has not yet arrived, having heard him in the witness box . . . As matters stand it would not be wise to release him on the business world.' The judge therefore granted Willie Stern his discharge but suspended it for another two and a half years – until September 1985.

Nobody emerges from the Stern affair with much credit. In lending Stern millions of pounds on nothing more substantial than his personal guarantee, the banks appear just as reckless and as foolish as Stern himself – if not more so. Legally Stern did nothing wrong: with the help of a rich and generous father he merely took advantage of a loophole in the law which smaller people are often too scrupulous, too badly advised, too confused or financially unable to use. Few are sufficiently prescient to anticipate bankruptcy two years in advance. Stern, on the other hand, had plenty of warning. Quite plainly, he is in a different league from the shopkeepers and engine drivers we met in Chapter Three. Their misfortune was that their debts were not so large as to be out of all reckoning and therefore they were made to pay and as a consequence lost everything.

Stern, by contrast, has lost comparatively little, at least in terms of comfort and lifestyle. Nobody has disconnected his telephone or intercepted his mail. He continues to earn what to most people would be a respectable salary and to live in a manner that is an affront to anyone with a sense of natural justice. How can the law, on the one hand, punish little people so severely yet let a man like Willie Stern off more or less scot free?

Stern is no criminal; he has broken no law, however distasteful his personal use of company money may have been. But if laws are to be respected and obeyed they should be fair and be seen to be fair. What offends in the Stern case is that there appears to be one law for the rich and the well-advised and quite another for the poor and confused. And what makes Stern's behaviour so open to criticism is that he deliberately and cynically took advantage of what to other, more scrupulous, folk might have seemed to be a crushing liability. He knew very well that his debts were so enormous that even if he worked for a thousand years he would never be able to pay them off.

From the start he realised that his bankruptcy was, in one sense, an elaborate charade. Only once in the course of a long court hearing was this basic fact acknowledged, and it was Stern himself who raised it. The exchange began when counsel for the creditors remarked mildly: 'It strikes some people as very odd that a man who has gone bankrupt for £100 million should go on living in a pretty substantial mansion.' 'Yes,' Stern replied, 'of that I'm acutely aware. It raises a severe public relations problem. But the value of the house is not an issue before the court. If it had been worth £10 million or £15 million it might have been different.'

This, it seems to me, is a most revealing remark which goes to the heart of the affair. In effect what he was saying was that there was not the faintest chance of paying off the money: so why bother? Even if he sold up entirely and moved into a council flat would it really make that much difference? And if not, why should his wife and children suffer?

In other words, Willie Stern has put his family and in the process himself first. His American relatives who have now put up close to £1 million have been remarkably generous but it is Stern, his wife and his children who have been the chief beneficiaries; the creditors have come a very poor second. In the process the law has been made to look very foolish. But as Stern himself would argue it would not be for the first time, and besides that is not his problem.

5 *The Undertakers*

WHEN IN January 1982 John DeLorean's Belfast sports car company finally ran out of cash, the man the British Government brought in to sort out the mess was Sir Kenneth Cork of W. H. Cork Gully, the City accountants. It was a logical choice. Sir Kenneth, then sixty-eight, was far and away Britain's best-known corporate undertaker. In more than thirty-five years in the trade he has presided over the last rites of many famous corporate funerals – John Bloom's Rolls Razor, Emil Savundra's Fire, Auto and Marine, Vehicle and General, the insurance company, and the property empires of Willie Stern and Ronnie Lyon. As it turned out Sir Kenneth failed to save DeLorean, but that was not his fault.

Cork is a name that, once linked to a company, can wipe millions off the share price overnight. Once when Cork was spotted during the great banking crisis of 1973 emerging from the Bank of England at dead of night, reportedly with a coat pulled over his head, it led to a story in *Accountancy Age*, the accountants' trade paper, that the Old Lady herself was in trouble.

Some months after the DeLorean crash, I was invited to a special performance laid on by the staff of Cork Gully for members of the Institute of Directors to explain the mysteries of insolvency. Over the years the firm, like Sir Kenneth himself, has developed a flair for showmanship. So instead of a series of solemn lectures by dark-suited accountants, the staff, which included Sir Kenneth's son Roger, presented a little play designed to show what happens to a company when the bank pulls the plug and the receiver moves in. The atmosphere was curiously light-hearted.

As the audience arrived Sir Kenneth, looking like a tall and distinguished owl, moved about the audience rather like a headmaster presenting the school play to the parents. 'Nobody comes out of this well,' he said. 'It's pretty frivolous but there is a bit of a message in it. It shows the trials and tribulations of the receiver from the other side. You will see how horrible you all are as creditors.'

The play itself was pretty dreadful. The 'actors' hammed up their parts, milking the script for laughs. But as adult education (and as a sales pitch for Cork Gully) it was remarkably effective. The message was that, contrary to popular myth, the receiver and his men are just ordinary professionals doing a difficult and necessary job under very trying circumstances. As Sir Kenneth had said, nobody (except perhaps the receiver) came out of it well: the bank manager was shown as complacent and ill-informed; the managing director as lazy and incompetent; and the creditors aggressive and greedy. The receiver himself was depicted as a hard nut with a heart of stone: he was, if necessary, prepared to bargain but appeals to his better nature were to no avail. Those creditors, like the bank, with a preferred title to the assets had no reason to complain. But the ordinary, unsecured creditors, the suppliers and the customers, were less fortunate.

The economy was still in deep recession, bankruptcies and company liquidations were running at record levels, so there was a good deal of interest in all this. Even so the well-dressed, prosperous-looking businessmen seemed, I thought, a little uneasy at being there. Corporate failure, like traffic accidents, is a spectacle that has its own horrid fascination but it is one that most people do not wish to be associated with too closely, at least not publicly.

THE RECEIVERS

Insolvency is a highly emotional subject. Months, even years after the event, many of those who have passed through the hands of the receiver still bear the scars. And there are few, even the toughest, who are able to recall the experience with tranquillity.

David Morrell, former chief executive of Mitchell Construction, which went into receivership in 1973 after running into problems on the Kariba dam project in Zambia, is still bitter. He says: 'I found the experience one which I wouldn't wish on anybody. It displays a ruthlessness and an insensitivity that most of us would have thought had died out in the nineteenth century. Senior managers who have since gone on to top positions in other parts of industry . . . felt totally contaminated, unworthy and unclean. Reduced to the status of mere things, they had to watch, unconsulted, while the products of their time and care were ripped apart without as much as a thought or a glance in their direction. Granted that insolvency, like undertaking, probably demands a special outlook and attitude of mind, is it really necessary to behave like this? The undertaker is at least equipped with a piece of paper which indicates that the body is incapable of further feeling.'

Receivership is of its nature a very sudden and brutal business. Overnight men who have spent their lives building or working for a company are stripped of all title and power: they lose their jobs, their offices, their secretaries, their company cars and all the other perks that help define identity and bolster self-esteem. One minute they may be running a multi-million pound concern: the next the entire enterprise is in the hands of some faceless accountant who is making all the decisions.

'The general opinion of insolvency receivers and liquidators,' Sir Kenneth told a *Financial Times* conference in 1982, 'is that they are an unnecessary evil put in for the sole purpose of earning a decent living for themselves and all they do is shut up the business and that is the end of that.' In fact receivership, unlike liquidation, does not necessarily mean that the company's life is at an end. There are dozens of firms, like for example Rolls Royce which crashed in 1971, which are still trading today though often in a very different form: Rolls-Royce's aero-engine business is now Government-owned, while the car firm is a subsidiary of Vickers.

It is this aspect of the work that most receivers, who are very sensitive about their poor image, prefer to stress. They like to see themselves not as undertakers but as company surgeons performing emergency operations; cutting out the diseased parts of the body corporate so that the healthy parts may live.

'We are here to save companies not to bury them,' says Cork. In 1965, Sir Kenneth got his first receivership. Barclays Bank had noticed how frequently the Cork name had figured in the *London Gazette* as liquidators and thought the time had come to try the firm out with something more ambitious. Kenneth and his brother Norman were summoned to lunch in the boardroom. After the inspection had been completed and the deal done, Barclays brought out the champagne. The firm in question was a now forgotten TV company called Peto Scott. And the job gave Cork an opportunity to demonstrate his go-getting abilities which had already made him such a name as a liquidator. Instead of closing the business down and selling off the assets, Cork took some of the company's TV sets down to the Radio Exhibition at Olympia, slashed the prices and cheekily set up a stand opposite one of the firm's main rivals, Philips Electrical. The dodge was successful. The sets sold so well and Philips was so impressed that it bought Peto Scott which became part of Pye of Cambridge, then a Philips subsidiary. 'That was when we realised the benefits of selling a business as a going concern,' says Sir Kenneth.

Several years later Cork used a somewhat similar technique with the Foden lorry firm, a famous company that had fallen on hard times. 'It was very extravagantly run,' says Cork. 'It used to make all its own back axles when it would have been cheaper to buy in, so it went bust. But the Ministry of Defence was very anxious, for military reasons connected with NATO, that it should be kept going. So we were asked to help. But the question was: who would buy it? Every lorry firm in England was in equally bad shape. Going up to the plant by train I saw fields full of unsold lorries so there was clearly not much help there. We wrote to all the obvious people: Ford, Mercedes, Volvo – but they all said no. So the only answer was to hire a consultant and tell him to find a company that was keen to get a NATO order, was anxious to diversify and for whom trucks were no more than a third of its existing business. He came up with only one firm: the American PACCAR, makers of Peterbilt and Kenworth trucks. So I sent a telex to PACCAR saying: "This you must buy." The first answer was no but the next day I was on the plane to New York and got them to change their minds; a decision they have not regretted.

'In the old days it was simple enough,' Sir Kenneth says. 'The receiver was appointed by the bank and his only job was to recover the money and then get the hell out of it. That's one approach and there are a lot of people who still practise it. The other is that the receiver is not just the agent of the bank but is acting for the entire company. And therefore he has a threefold objective: to recover the bank's money; to get something for the creditors; and, if possible, to keep the company going. We have a duty to everybody: we have no more duty to the debenture holders than anyone else.'

Sir Kenneth never misses an opportunity to bring home this message. 'It is the business that must be saved,' he told a City audience in 1982, 'not necessarily the company – the company is something quite different; that has failed and need not be rescued. The business is the asset, and the business is the management, the work force who put their skills into it and the property of the people who supply it. If it gets shut – and there is nothing easier than to shut a business – it is lost and gone for ever.'

Fine words: but it must always be remembered that whatever his long-term objectives, legally the receiver's prime duty is to the debenture holder, usually the bank: it is the bank that appoints him under the terms of the debenture and it is the bank's money that he is obliged to recover. Whether he does it by closing the business or by selling it off in whole or part is up to him. Once installed the receiver is virtually impregnable. He is the boss and his decisions are almost always final. The company itself and the creditors are in no position to challenge them.

Theoretically the receiver can be sued by the company for maladministration or malpractice but as the directors or the liquidator acting on their behalf have to find the money to mount such an action, in practice this rarely happens. Also, astonishingly, the receiver is not obliged to account in any detail for his actions. There is no independent audit at the end of the day and receivers' reports to the Department of Trade and Industry are sketchy, to say the least. Furthermore there is no need to prove that assets have been sold off at a fair market price nor does the receiver have to justify, except to the bank, a decision to sell the company back to its previous owners. Directors frequently complain that the assets of the company have been sold off for a fraction of their real value. Receivers reply that this is one of the inevitable penalties of going bust: asset values are not absolute, they argue, they depend very much on whether or not the company is a going concern. It is an argument that leads to a great deal of bad feeling but as matters stand there is no mechanism for testing it.

The receiver's job is to satisfy the bank and everything else is, strictly speaking, incidental. It is not an easy job and it is not without risk: technically the receiver is personally liable for all debts he incurs. But he will always be insured and, throughout, the bank will be looking over his shoulder.

One of the strange and very British characteristics of the whole business is how much is based on custom and practice rather than statute – which is one reason why the accountants rather than the lawyers, as in America, dominate the business. As the *Economist* said in 1983: 'British bankrupts are best off because the foundations of today's British insolvency laws were laid in the second half of the nineteenth century, during the great Victorian commercial boom. The problems of financial collapse were seen in commercial, rather than in legal terms. So insolvency proceedings can be started voluntarily by a harassed debtor, controlled by his creditors, or run by more or less anyone who cares to make a grab for the business. The courts need never get a look in.' After a hundred years of benign neglect the Government is now trying to stamp out the worst abuses (see Chapters Six and Seven). But many of the more far-reaching reforms of the Cork Report have been ignored; the structure remains essentially Victorian; and there are still plenty of loopholes for the unscrupulous.

The vast majority of receivers these days are professional

accountants who owe their living to the banks who call them in to collect monies due by means of a curious and uniquely British device known as 'the floating charge'. This much-criticised instrument is the invention, not of the banks, but of the Court of Chancery and dates from the 1860s. An exact description has baffled lawyers for generations but put simply it is a mortgage secured against both present and *future* assets of the company: only when the receiver is appointed and the money called in does the charge, in legal language, 'crystallise'. It is then the receiver's job to realise the assets and pay off the creditors in strict rotation.

The preferred creditors such as the receiver himself, the Revenue and the VATman are served first; then comes the debenture holder (i.e. the bank) and only if anything is left over do the poor unsecured creditors get a look in. This is another reason why receivers are generally none too popular. By the time the receiver has done his work and the company goes into liquidation (a process I shall describe later) there are often few pickings left for the liquidator to distribute to the unsecured creditors. Only when a company goes straight into liquidation without passing through the hands of the receiver is the prospect at all bright.

Professional receivers plan the take-over with military precision. On the day a big company goes into receivership there are suddenly accountants everywhere. The receiver himself usually moves into the managing director's office, the finance director is given a thorough grilling, teams burrow through the company's books, and men are posted at all entrances to make sure that in the confusion nobody makes off with anything of any conceivable value. 'It is essential,' says Bill Mackey of Ernst and Whinney in his guide to receivership, 'to man all points of entry to the factory or works. Wherever possible the receiver must use his own staff. He can help himself by reducing the number of receiving points. Instructions to administrative staff not to accept goods without his sanction must be given in writing and he should list the names of his staff who are authorised to accept delivery. I always ask the company's staff to sign copies of the instructions indicating that they have read and understood them and will comply with them . . . The receiver must protect the company and himself from incurring further liability.'

Like many top-flight receivers Mackey does not fit the traditional image of the accountant. A hard-bitten, no-nonsense Geordie he joined the Navy aged seventeen and had an adventurous war as a commando with a mini-submarine unit, raiding the ports of Nazi-occupied France. After the war he worked for a time for the Inland Revenue, chasing debtors – work which he found surprisingly congenial. 'What I liked about it was the element of personal confrontation,' he says. 'You would sit the man down on the other side of the table and try and get him to tell you the truth. Often they wouldn't want to tell you. There are usually things they want to hide, like they are keeping a mistress or something. But it would be my job to find out; to break the man apart.' A confessed insomniac – 'I can get by with very little sleep' – Mackey sees himself as a man of action with a decidedly sardonic view of British industry.

One of his party pieces is a recital of the danger signs of an impending crash. Beware, he says: of Rolls Royces with personalised number plates; of fountains in the reception area; of salesmen and engineers as chief executives; of firms who have recently moved into modern offices; and of chairmen who are politicians or well known for charitable works.

Mackey himself is a workaholic. 'There is nothing clever about receivership work but you do have to be totally committed to it.' His only relaxation is the opera and his cottage in the Dordogne; though even there, there is a private airstrip so that he can return to London at a moment's notice. In 1982 Ernst and Whinney handled more receiverships than any other firm (469 to Cork Gully's 197). And as the recently promoted head of the firm's UK operation, Mackey probably earns more than £100,000 a year.

To see how a typical receivership works let's look at the fate of Dragon Data, a computer firm which first flourished and then failed during the extraordinary home computer boom of the early eighties. Launched in August 1982 as an offshoot of

Mettoy, the toy firm which itself crashed some months later, Dragon produced a well-made but not exactly state-of-the-art, inexpensive computer for the domestic market – selling through Boots and Dixons.

The company first ran into difficulties in the summer of 1983 when it suffered a cash flow crisis – the result of over-optimism. There were not enough sales to finance the very heavy stock build-up. To save the company a £4.5 million rescue package was arranged.

But everything still depended on the forthcoming Christmas. Just as the company was gearing up for Christmas it was hit by the worldwide shortage of micro chips – the 'heart' of any computer. The Dragon was driven by a Motorola 6809 micro processor for which there was a six-month waiting list. So production was badly hit; and as sales dropped the distributors, Boots and Dixons, unilaterally lopped £50 off the price and then asked Dragon to make good the loss and restore the margin. Dragon's problem was that it did not have its own distribution network and was entirely in the hands of the retailers.

The Christmas sales were not all that bad, though lower than expected. The real problem came a couple of months later, early in 1984, when sales dropped away completely. Not only was no cash coming in, but the products were nearing the end of their life and enormous sums were needed to finance new products and keep the company in the game. Nobody thought this was realistic, especially the backers. And at the end of May 1984 the company, at the request of Hill Samuel, called in Touche Ross as receivers. The accountants knew the score as they had already done an investigation at the bank's request.

The receiver, Robert Ellis, says his approach was a gentle one. 'In the old days we would have arrived with half a dozen people and banged about with heavy boots. In fact I only took one person with me to my first meeting with the directors. The atmosphere was quite friendly.' Ellis makes it sound as if he was some kind of psychoanalyst rather than an executioner. 'The object,' he says, 'was to get the directors to talk about their feelings. The great art of receivers is to get the directors to unburden themselves. You see, the receiver has to judge whether or not he can rely on the directors. There are all kinds of decisions that have to be made: should we close down the business, or should we continue to trade; and if so, how much will it cost? The great aim is to package up the assets and then sell it all off, if you possibly can, as a going concern.

'As a receiver you are entirely on your own. Your powers are enormous and there are virtually no checks, apart from your own company's internal ones, on what you are doing. In theory the liquidator can challenge your actions and hold you to account but it's not very effective, partly because a liquidator is not always appointed, and partly because he always arrives after the event when the damage, if any, has already been done.'

Ellis says the break-up of Dragon proved to be a remarkably simple exercise – a classic receivership. The staff was reduced from 150 to 80 within two days – all the hourly-paid staff, mostly women, were fired the very day they came back from their annual holiday. The only people to keep their jobs were the senior managers, the design team and the technical staff. Another couple of dozen were retained to do the stock-taking but once that job was completed, they too were fired. Professional valuers were hired to put two sets of prices on the assets: one, as a going concern, and the other, as a forced sale. A sales brochure was prepared, the company was advertised in the *Financial Times* and the *Daily Telegraph*, the two papers most favoured by receivers, and then Ellis sat back and waited for offers. In the event there were only three takers: Britain's General Electric Company, America's Tandy Corporation and, from Spain, a new government-backed concern called Eurohard SA, formed to promote industrial development in Estremadura, one of Spain's most backward regions. Two months later Eurohard emerged as the successful bidder.

It is hard not to feel some sympathy both for Dragon and the Welsh. It was a brave though misguided attempt to bring high technology to the valleys and ease the burden of unemployment as the coal industry ran down.

There is a lot of money to be made out of receiverships and

liquidations. Insolvency, for so long the Cinderella of the accountancy world, is these days a multi-million pound business with an annual turnover, I would estimate, of over £50 million. (It has to be a guess as the Department of Trade no longer publishes full statistics.) It is, of course, a much riskier business than auditing, where the work is steady and the income guaranteed. Auditing remains the bread and butter, occupying about 80 per cent of the accountants' time. But over the past ten years or so insolvency work has expanded so much that today it is one of the most lucrative sides of the business.

When questioned about their profits most firms tend to be rather coy and, as most are partnerships, details are sparse. 'Let's say that we would be all right even if we didn't do another pennyworth of business for the next three years,' says Keith Goodman of Leonard Curtis. The pace is set by the Department of Trade and Industry which lays down a scale of fees for compulsory liquidations which is used by the profession as a guide: on monies recovered it is 20 per cent for the first £5000, 15 per cent for the next £5000, 10 per cent for sums up to £90,000 and 5 per cent thereafter. The receiver or liquidator also collects on monies paid out, though the rewards here are less generous; roughly half. Most of the big firms, however, prefer to charge on a time basis with a set fee for each member of the firm, depending on seniority. Thus a senior partner will cost £50 or £60 an hour and so on down the scale. In a big complicated case like the winding up of the Savings Investment Bank of the Isle of Man which Cork Gully handled jointly with Peat, Marwick, Mitchell, Cork Gully's own share came to well over £200,000.

In fact receivers often charge what they think the market will bear. 'It's obviously stupid to overcharge the bank because you depend on them for repeat business,' says the partner of one well-known Manchester firm. 'But once the bank has been assured that it will get its money back they are generally not too fussy about the fees.'

It is a very grey area. And even some of the most respectable firms cannot sometimes resist the temptation to supplement their income. One of the lesser known perks of the business is the commission, normally one per cent, paid out by building societies to large investors. The rate of return may not be as high as could be obtained elsewhere. But for a receiver or liquidator with £100,000 in the kitty, the extra £1000 in the firm's account can come in very handy.

Liquidators who, unlike receivers, are appointed by and responsible to the creditors, are in theory more closely supervised. Their fees are supposed to be vetted and approved by a creditors' committee of inspection. But such bodies are not mandatory and even when they are appointed the members are usually more concerned to get their money back than in vetting the liquidator's fees. As we shall see in Chapter Six this is one of the many weaknesses in the system which has been exploited by the 'cowboy' liquidators.

Insolvency is a specialised business requiring very different skills and personalities from regular accountancy. None of the top receivers or liquidators I met struck me, except in matters of dress where they were uniformly neat and tidy, to fit the book-keeping image of the traditional accountant. They seemed to enjoy the uncertainty, the freedom and the power and were not men who were easily crossed or would enjoy losing an argument. 'It's not a game where you are adding up figures and making them agree,' says Pat White of Booth, White and president of the Insolvency Practitioners Association. 'You have to be an extrovert, fairly unflappable and have an ability to get on with everybody.'

It is a small, tight-knit world where everybody knows what everybody else is up to. Most firms have their own network of formal and informal contacts. Many of those in the insolvency business are, like Sir Kenneth Cork himself, Freemasons. 'I keep getting these very strange handshakes,' says Sir Kenneth's brother, the unmasonic Norman Cork. The undertakers have their own closed shop, the Insolvency Practitioners Association, which was founded some twenty years ago by Bob Hellyer, an accountant and ex-Japanese prisoner of war from Leeds, to bring some respectability to a business whose image was rather tarnished. The IPA, which now has some ninety members including all the big firms, has all the apparatus of a fully fledged professional body. It sets examinations, vets potential members, and, very discreetly, disciplines the black sheep. But the formal qualifications of many of the older members are minimal. Even today a good percentage of the IPA membership, including its current president, Pat White ('Somehow I never managed to finish the exams'), are not qualified accountants. There is an annual dinner in the City to which leading members of the bankruptcy bar are invited and in the early spring the members fly off for a week to some sunny place to exchange notes at their annual conference.

The receivers are the aristocrats of the business. Few earn less than £50,000 a year. And some are paid a good deal more than that. Sir Kenneth Cork is not only the most eminent practitioner in the field but he is also the richest. His firm, W. H. Cork Gully, which merged with Cooper Brothers in 1983, does not, like most accountants, publish a break-down of its profits. But it is safe to say that Sir Kenneth is a millionaire several times over. He drives a Rolls Royce, lives in Great Missenden in Buckinghamshire; and when he became Lord Mayor of London (never a post for a poor man) he spent £50,000 of his own money during his term of office. It is an indication of Cork Gully's standing in the City (and also perhaps of its profits) that the firm has already provided two Lord Mayors. And as Sir Kenneth's son Roger is now an alderman it looks set for a third. Sir Kenneth's brother Norman, who worked for the firm for more than twenty years, told me that at his peak in the mid-sixties he was handling over 1000 liquidations a year and had an annual income of over £200,000. Some of it came from property investments in Turkey and Malta where he had a part share with Baron von Richthofen in an hotel called the Dragonara but the bulk was earned from his commissions as Cork Gully's chief drummer. As Norman failed to complete his accountancy exams he never became a partner in the firm, so he was paid a small salary plus commission on work that he brought in.

For years the established firms like Peat, Marwick, Mitchell and Cooper Brothers who had grown fat on auditing over the previous half century shunned insolvency work. They thought it was rather grubby. Apart from the occasional big receivership they left the work to be scrambled for by a handful of highly entrepreneurial specialists like Bernard Phillips, Stoy Hayward, and Leonard Curtis, whose outlook and background was very different to the dignified, status-conscious leaders of the profession, the Peats, the Deloittes and the Coopers. It is no accident that many of these smaller firms are Jewish in origin and they owed much of their early success to their close contacts with the rag trade in which insolvency is endemic. Bankruptcy is part of the mythology of the Jewish rag trade, the subject of many jokes. One of the favourites, still told in the streets around the Middlesex Hospital, just north of Oxford Circus, where the rag trade now has its headquarters after moving from the East End in the 1920s, concerns two traders who meet to exchange news.

'I hear that you have gone bankrupt,' said the first.

'Yes,' said the second. 'The creditors meet tomorrow.'

'The house? Surely that's in the wife's name?' inquired the first.

'No.'

'The business? Surely the assets have been transferred?'

'No. I've given personal guarantees.'

'Well,' said the friend. 'In that case you are not bankrupt, you are *mechuleh* – destroyed.'

Gradually the big battalions began to realise that they were missing out on an extraordinarily profitable line of business. It was also good for contacts and kept them in the public eye – an important point for a profession which was forbidden, at least in theory, to advertise. And so from about the mid-sixties onwards the big firms began to set up their own 'coffin and shroud' departments, as they are known in the trade. Either talent was brought in from the smaller firms or the firms themselves were taken over: Arthur Anderson, for example, merged with Bernard Phillips while Cooper Brothers merged with Cork Gully.

The breakthrough came in 1971 when Rupert Nicholson of Peat, Marwick, Mitchell was appointed joint receiver of Rolls Royce – the first time the Corks had lost out for as long as anybody could remember. But since then the big firms, thanks to the close links with the banks, have strengthened their hold on the receivership end of the market. The league table of receivers' appointments published by Dun and Bradstreet shows that some nine firms dominate the business. Here are the figures for 1982:

Ernst and Whinney	469
Peat, Marwick, Mitchell	387
Thornton Baker	354
Price Waterhouse	214
Cork Gully	197
Touche Ross	171
Spicer & Pegler	169
Deloittes	104
Arthur Andersen	102
Stoy Hayward	87
Arthur Young	87
Total	2341
Others	1097
Total	3438

What the figures also reveal is the pattern of bank patronage. Some banks, like Barclays, dispensed their favours fairly evenly between five or six firms while the Midland gave nearly a third of its entire business for 1982 to one firm: Ernst and Whinney, who are also the bank's auditors.

THE LIQUIDATORS

If the receivers are the aristocrats of the profession, then the liquidators are the journeymen. Of Sir Kenneth Cork one distinguished practitioner said to me: 'He's a lovely man but he remains a liquidator at heart.'

The technicalities are formidable and baffling – a jungle through which the unscrupulous have learned to cut some very profitable paths. But there is no mystery about what a liquidator does. Technically, he is appointed by the shareholders and is called in when all hope has gone; his job is simply to wind up the company and distribute whatever assets remain. Sometimes the receiver has been there before him in which case the pickings are usually slim; on other occasions where the company has gone straight into liquidation the job can be more rewarding.

During the bankruptcy boom of the early 1980s it was not uncommon for single firms to have several hundred liquidations on the books at any one time. Booth, White is one of the smaller, old-established firms which has been in business since around 1850. It has Dickensian offices in the shadow of St Paul's. In 1983 it handled 150 separate liquidations on which it earned, so the chairman, Pat White, says, an average fee of £4000, which puts the annual turnover at around £600,000. That of a big firm like Cork Gully with forty-nine insolvency specialists on the staff is probably ten times as large.

The origins even of some of the City's most famous names are somewhat rough and ready. The history of Cork Gully, for example, goes back to the turn of the century. The firm was founded by Sir Kenneth's father, William Henry, who was forced to leave school at the age of fourteen after his father, Sir Kenneth's grandfather, nearly wrecked the family's finances by imprudently guaranteeing a friend's overdraft. Young William Henry was hired at five shillings a week by one Oscar Berry who specialised in bankruptcies and liquidations – the sort of work that no respectable accountant in those days would touch. Berry was a man of a somewhat nervous disposition: the firm had offices just below the Monument in the City and Berry took out an insurance policy to cover him in case the Monument fell on the office; needless to say the premium was very small.

In 1906, when he was twenty-one, William Henry left Berry's to set up on his own as the official liquidator to the Grocery Merchants and Allied Traders, the trade association of the grocery business. As grocery shops were as prone to bankruptcy then as they are now, business was brisk and surprisingly all-embracing. William Henry was more than just the liquidator: he was valuer, auctioneer, estate agent and liquidator all rolled into one. In those days conflict of interest was of less pressing concern than it is now. In addition to his salary from the trade association young Cork also earned fees and commissions from his liquidations.

His career was interrupted by World War One in which he fought as a member of the Essex Regiment. But on his return he set up at 15 Eastcheap with another liquidator called Oliver Sunderland. His big break came when he was asked by the then Ministry of Food to auction off the army's surplus food supplies. Work also came from the International Tea Stores (now International Stores, recently sold by British American Tobacco) for whom he acted as a purchasing agent. William Henry would tour the country looking for likely prospects: small, profitable, family grocery businesses. He was a shrewd and hard bargainer. He told one shopkeeper: 'Mr Jones, even if you covered the door of your shop with diamonds, I wouldn't give you a better price for it.'

In 1935 William Henry joined forces with Gully and Co, then run by a man who was later to die in a shooting accident in which his wife, it is said, was also involved. The business was doing sufficiently well for Cork to send his two sons, Kenneth and Norman, to school at Berkhamsted and to maintain a house in Finchley, North London. But at about the time Cork Gully was formed disaster struck again. William Henry had taken over as liquidator the affairs of a gramophone company. But instead of closing the business down he tried to carry on the company himself. This proved to be a bad decision. The first radiograms were just coming on to the market, demand for gramophones slumped, and William Henry found himself with a large stock of unsaleable gramophones. The family was not ruined but the episode made a nasty hole in its finances. By the outbreak of World War Two William Henry was seriously ill. He died of cancer in 1940 – a comparatively poor man.

His sons, Kenneth and Norman, may not have come into much money but they both, plainly, inherited their father's entrepreneurial flair. The young Corks were also energetic and ambitious. And when they returned from the war in which they served with the Honourable Artillery Company they set about reviving the somewhat moribund family business. According to Norman, Kenneth, anxious to make his way in the City, regarded insolvency work as somewhat infra dig. He was already a qualified accountant and wanted to build up a solid, conventional practice. Norman, a more flamboyant, free-wheeling character than his brother, was more impatient. He says that when Kenneth asked him what he wanted to do, he replied: 'Make money in the City.' And then what? 'Make more money.' And so while Kenneth looked after the books, brother Norman tramped the streets looking for ways to revive the business.

The first sign that he was heading in the right direction came in the winter of 1948/49 when the firm got its first big liquidation job, on which it earned £15,000 in fees – big money in those days.

Liquidation jobs, then as now, were not easy to come by: they had to be scrambled for. The easiest route is via the company itself. Often when a company is in trouble the directors will decide to call in a liquidator themselves, and if he decides that the company is indeed insolvent, then it will be wound up. Rather confusingly this process is known as 'a creditors' voluntary liquidation' even though it is the directors that make the decision on behalf of the shareholders, not the creditors. One of its curious features is that although the liquidator is in charge from the moment he is called in, his appointment has no legal force until it has been approved at a creditors' meeting. Under Section 293, sub-section 1, of the 1948 Companies Act this should be held within twenty-four hours of the board's decision to wind up. Failure to do so carries a penalty of £100. But in practice this rarely happens: normally at least three weeks elapse between the arrival of the acting liquidator and the creditors' meeting. And once the liquidator is in place it can prove very difficult to dislodge him.

Until recently accountants were forbidden by their Institute either to advertise or to tout for business. But that did not prevent them from setting up their own highly efficient early warning system which enabled them to pick up the gossip. Most firms specialise: Cork Gully knows all about the grocery trade, Booth, White is expert in the drinks and paper business, while Leonard Curtis is known as a specialist in the rag trade. Through membership of the appropriate trade association and by lunches with firms' credit managers, the liquidators can build

up a shrewd and well-informed idea of what is going on the
market and what the next job might be: how big, how profitable
and, most important, what the competition is likely to be.
Accountants like to make out that they are disinterested professionals acting solely on behalf of the creditors but in fact they
fight fiercely among themselves for business. But if the competition is too heavy they will sometimes agree, rather than slug it
out at the creditors' meeting, to divide the work among themselves by arranging a joint liquidation. 'I wouldn't describe it as
a carve-up,' says Spicer and Pegler's Richard Turton. 'But let's
say that in most cases it is all arranged beforehand.'

Even so the battle is not won unless and until their appointment is approved at the creditors' meeting – which is why these
can be lively, noisy and sometimes hilarious affairs. Some days
before the meeting the creditors will have sent in their proxy
forms nominating the liquidator of their choice. The rule is that
the job goes to the man who obtains a majority by both number
and value. In theory therefore the result should be a foregone
conclusion. But because there are almost always some uncom-
mitted creditors at the meeting there is ample scope for a bit of
persuasive advocacy.

Professional rules forbid accountants to vote for themselves.
But in the past many firms have got round this problem by
employing freelance 'meetings men'. 'For a big out-of-town
liquidation,' says Richard Turton, 'everybody used to turn up.
There would be ten people from London and another dozen
from the sticks, all yelling their heads off. It was all rather
degrading.'

Degrading it may have been but for the old school of
insolvency men, like Norman Cork, uninhibited by membership
of any professional body, it was one of the most enjoyable parts
of the business. 'It was the greatest possible fun: pure theatre,'
he recalls. 'I always sat at the back and did my best to tear holes
in everybody's arguments.' Norman would frequently interrupt
to put his opponents off their stroke. On one occasion a rival
liquidator, a very short man, was addressing the meeting when
Norman boomed out: 'Mr Chairman, would you kindly ask that
man in the front to stand up, please.' 'But he is already standing

up,' the chairman replied to general laughter. 'It was,' Norman Cork says, 'a business with plenty of bullshit and not much knowledge.' Cork's chief adversary was Leonard Curtis who has now retired and lives much of the year in Spain. For years the two men had an agreement that the winner would buy the loser a bottle of champagne as a consolation prize. In this fashion much money was made and much champagne consumed.

These days creditors' meetings tend to be rather more sober affairs. With the entry of the big firms the style is cooler, more professional and less buccaneering. But it remains for all that a rough, tough business.

6 *The Cowboys*

ONE FRIDAY AFTERNOON in the early winter of 1983 three soberly dressed men could be seen in earnest discussion in the lobby of the plush Metropole Hotel which is part of Birmingham's National Exhibition Centre. The hotel has been built for businessmen, and much of its trade comes from the hiring out of its rooms for private meetings. On the surface it all looked very tranquil. The coffee shop was doing brisk business and the restaurant was taking last orders for lunch.

The three men, all insolvency experts, represented some of the best-known accounting firms in the country: Spicer and Pegler's Lindsay Denney had driven over from Nottingham, Thornton Baker's Geoffrey Harrison had come from Birmingham and Cork Gully had sent its own man on the afternoon train up from London. All had come at short notice and the reason they were there was that word had gone out that a Birmingham-based company called Joan Scott Consultancy Ltd had made arrangements for at least six companies to be wound up that day and for a liquidator to be appointed. The man put forward for the job was the same Birmingham accountant in every case.

The three accountants were representing the creditors of a small company called Holmes Wheatland which made catering equipment for schools and hospitals. It was based 150 miles away at Wantage in Oxfordshire and had decided to go into voluntary liquidation three weeks before. The professionals knew nothing about the company except that it was insolvent and owed their clients money – sums ranging from £4000 to 69p. So, after exchanging notes, they moved off to the York Room in search of enlightenment.

The room was empty apart from three people, seated at a bare table and looking nervous and uncomfortable. There was a middle-aged couple who turned out to be Mr and Mrs Brian Barrett, the owners of the failed company, and a man in his early forties who was chain-smoking and wearing a light grey suit. He was, he explained, the acting liquidator.

The meeting got off to a bad start – thanks largely to the absence of the firm's managing director who had, it emerged, taken a new job and therefore could not be there to face the creditors. It was left to a bewildered Mrs Barrett to do the best she could in what were to prove rather trying circumstances.

The firm had failed, she explained, because of the recession which led to cut-backs in the schools and hospitals which had been the firm's main customers. 'We kept hoping that something would turn up but somehow it never did,' she said apologetically.

A statement of affairs, prepared by the acting liquidator, was then handed round. It was a bleak and singularly uninformative document, no more than a single sheet of paper. It showed merely that the firm's debts exceeded its assets by some £35,000. But how had the firm got into this position? When was it set up? What was its trading record? Where were the audited accounts? The questions from the professionals came thick and fast. The liquidator explained that unfortunately he had left most of the papers behind in London. And it was only gradually that the full picture emerged.

About three weeks earlier, quite out of the blue, the company had had a call from somebody from Joan Scott. The caller explained that he understood the company was in trouble and as he represented a firm of consultants that specialised in helping companies in difficulties perhaps he could come and see them? He talked vaguely about helping out with the marketing. The Barretts were a little puzzled. They had not advertised their difficulties and were at a loss to know why a firm in Birmingham of which they had never heard should be taking such an interest in a little company like theirs so far away. 'Perhaps they just picked us out of the Yellow Pages,' said Mr Barrett. Nevertheless the Barretts agreed and soon afterwards the real purpose of the call became clear.

Going Bust

After the briefest of inspections the Barretts were advised that their position was hopeless and that the best thing they could do was to wind the company up. They had no need to worry: the Joan Scott Consultancy would arrange everything. Its appointee was standing by to take over as liquidator, a statement of affairs would be prepared, a creditors' meeting summoned and finally Joan Scott would see to it that the monies due to the firm, some £12,000, would be collected. To the Barretts, confused and bewildered, it seemed a reasonable deal and so they said: 'We just stopped and handed everything over to Joan Scott.'

But the accountants were still not satisfied. 'Why,' they wanted to know, 'was the firm's plant and equipment listed in the statement of affairs as being worth only £2,800 when only a year ago they were valued at £9,500? Could it be,' they inquired innocently, 'that Mr Barrett was thinking of starting up all over again?' 'Well, yes,' Mr Barrett replied. 'I did have something of the kind in mind.' The accountants did not pursue this point. Their aim was to oppose the appointment of the liquidator; not that they had anything against him personally but simply because he was acting on behalf of Joan Scott, an old adversary.

In the end they won on a technical knock-out. As the official chairman of the meeting, the absent managing director, had not bothered to attend, the proxy votes that would have given the acting liquidator the job did not count. And so the accountants, representing the creditors, won the day. It was agreed that the man from Cork Gully should take over. 'Theoretically we are competitors,' said Spicer and Pegler's Lindsay Denney over a cup of tea afterwards. 'I don't normally like to give a job to the opposition. But in cases like this we tend to work together.'

While in this case all went well and the accountants were merely being cautious, there have been other cases where the creditors of small companies have been startled and hood-winked by unscrupulous operators. 'There is a web of cavalier insolvency practitioners in Britain,' said Bernard Phillips, the outgoing chairman of the Insolvency Practitioners Association which was set up twenty years ago largely in an attempt to control the cowboys. 'They are well known to me and I'm well known to them. These bounders milk the owners of companies and the creditors and have blackened the name of insolvency practice.'

This is not a new problem. Making money out of other people's misfortunes has always been a popular and highly profitable pastime for the less scrupulous. And there is a particular type of person who makes a fat living, feeding off the bodies of insolvent companies. In 1879 the Comptroller in Bankruptcy described the activities of the rogue liquidators as 'an organised system of plunder'. One firm, he said, operated 'in a manner so bare-faced, that it would seem incredible to anyone who was not habitually conversant with the state of things which exists under the present bankruptcy system . . . the present system leaves thousands of cases to be scrambled for and in such a scramble the most unscrupulous are generally the most successful.'

What was true in 1879 remains just as true today. As we have already seen in the last chapter liquidation can be a highly profitable business, even for the most scrupulous and professional of operators. But the cowboys charge all along the line: there is the initial 'consultation' fee which can be as much as £1000; then comes the fee for preparing the statement of affairs; then the standard percentage charge on assets realised; and, finally, quite often, a backhander from the directors who have bought back the assets at a knock-down price.

But the game does not necessarily stop there: frequently the rogue liquidator, as we shall see, will grab the assets within hours of his appointment and sell them at a notional price to nominee companies controlled by himself or his friends. This is a very crude manoeuvre. But many of the cowboys now employ much more sophisticated techniques. They have mastered every twist and turn of company law to keep creditors at bay. And they have become experts in the black art of shuffling debts and assets in such a way as to enable seemingly bankrupt companies to rise phoenix-like from the ashes to everyone's advantage, save the creditors'. 'We know the insolvency laws backwards,' Maurice Sidney Caplan, better known as Hissing Sid, told Colin Simpson of *The Sunday Times* in April 1981. 'They are so loose and flexible that we can drive a coach and horses through them.'

Going Bust

Hissing Sid gets his nickname from a cartoon character fashionable in the early eighties. But his notoriety stems from the fact that he has been one of the most active and most ambitious of the cowboys. His earliest adventures were in the rag trade. When still only twenty-five he formed a company called V. E. Hosiers Ltd which was wound up by the courts in 1949. Six years later the same fate befell another of his companies, Direct Mills Supplies Ltd. But he was not deterred. Throughout the sixties companies came and went and in each case the pattern was the same. The only people who seemed to suffer from these repeated liquidations were the creditors. Altogether ten of Sid's companies with such exotic names as Fabulous Fashions Ltd and Fabulous Suedes Ltd went into liquidation and in 1968 Sid himself was declared bankrupt until his eventual discharge ten years later. In the meantime he had served an eighteen-month prison sentence for carrying on a finance company with an intent to defraud creditors and had also had a conviction for handling stolen goods. In 1983 the Department of Trade and Industry moved to wind up his company, Chancery Lane Registrars, after a two-year investigation; and in January 1984 he was convicted at Manchester Crown Court for falsifying company documents. He was fined £5000 and given a nine-month suspended sentence.

His own company was originally called Rapid Registrars Ltd, but on October 25, 1978, the name was changed to Chancery Lane Registrars, which operated from a suite of offices near Liverpool Street Station. Caplan's partners were two men whose business careers were as chequered as his own: Paul Davies, a suspended solicitor, who has been fined £1000 for uttering a forged document, and Stephen Pepler, who acted as the company's unqualified accountant and who has served eighteen months for attempting to defraud some leading banks, among them Nat West, Barclays and the Midland.

Unlike many of the operators Chancery Lane was not a one-man band: it was a highly integrated operation with its own legal and financial services. It also had a half share in a company called London and Bedford (Realisations) Ltd which, quite improperly, did much of the company's inventory and valuation work. Legally, a liquidator is required to keep the accounts of each job quite separate. But that was not Chancery Lane's style. All the money flowed back into the common pot in such a way that the DTI investigators found it difficult to tell what sums belonged to which company. 'The company has in effect,' the DTI concluded, 'been carrying out the liquidations and receiverships itself with the nominal liquidators or receivers being either mere figureheads or creatures of the company . . . Particularly objectionable is the handling of the monies and other assets of companies in liquidation by another limited company. The very nature of the company's business is open to this fundamental objection and would be so even if the highest standards of prudence and accounting rectitude had been maintained.' The inspectors found that money belonging to more than two hundred liquidated companies had been channelled to Chancery Lane and that the whole enterprise was little more than a vehicle for the enrichment of Hissing Sid and his friends.

The process of winding up a company is often complex and hedged about with all kinds of rules and restrictions. The basic instrument, the 1948 Companies Act, has, for example, no fewer than 166 detailed sections, studded with sub-clauses, setting out the procedures and dealing with every contingency. But though the duties and the powers of the receiver and the liquidator are minutely prescribed there was, until the Government's recent legislation, one glaring omission: anybody could set up as a receiver or liquidator, provided he was not himself a bankrupt or was otherwise disqualified from acting as a director of a company. As receivers are invariably appointed by banks, only qualified accountants usually get a look in. But with liquidators who operate at the grubby end of the trade it is quite another story. There are, so the Insolvency Practitioners Association reckons, at least twenty firms which as a matter of course take more than full advantage of the freedom the liquidator enjoys. Few people realise how much scope for mischief the law allows. In many cases, even before his appointment has been confirmed by the creditors, the acting liquidator is in sole charge. It is he who decides before or after his actual appointment whether assets should be sold and if so at what price; and which creditors should be paid and how much. Once the company is in the hands of the liquidator the previous directors are powerless. If they have been propositioned and later cheated they are often too embarrassed or too compromised to blow the whistle. In theory the liquidator is answerable to the creditors, who theoretically ratify his appointment. But it is, as we shall see, often all too easy for a cunning and determined liquidator to frustrate creditors' attempts to throw him out. But the most important thing is to get the foot in the door.

THE LIQUIDATOR CALLS

It is rare for him to make the first approach. That is the job of a special breed of operators who advertise widely in the Sunday newspapers, offering companies in trouble a way out of their difficulties. They usually describe themselves as company advisers or management consultants. Their real rôle, however, is to act as scouts for the cowboys who pay them a commission. The Department of Trade's investigation of Chancery Lane revealed that the firm employed a whole network of agents in the south east, in the Midlands and in the north of England who in addition to placing advertisements in the papers, combed the pages of the *London Gazette* and *Stubbs Gazette* looking for likely prospects. In a single year Chancery Lane paid out nearly £30,000 to its agents.

Out of the blue, a company on the brink of closure will get a letter something like this:

> Dear Sir or Madam,
> Are you aware that your business is listed as a debtor in a recent publication? Could this be an indication of problems being experienced? We apologise if you feel that we have misunderstood the situation, but as established Insolvency Practitioners and Management Consultants we would be pleased to offer you the opportunity to discuss the Facilities listed below . . .

Insolvent companies are offered 'advice regarding personal guarantees' and what are delicately described as 'the various methods of Survival [sic] available to senior management'. The prevailing tone is, however, always upbeat, for the scouts like to present themselves as lifesavers, not undertakers.

At Christmas 1982, Roger Porter, the owner of a garage business on the Isle of Dogs on the River Thames, was at home in Blackheath idly reading through *The Sunday Times* when he noticed an advertisement: 'Company directors with problems. We arrange advice and help,' it said. For Porter it was not a happy Christmas. His wife was in hospital for an operation; his eldest son had seriously hurt his hand in an accident with a food mixer; and the business, started in 1968, was in trouble. 'It was beginning to lose money,' Porter said. 'I already owed the bank £34,000 and I knew that if I went on like this I would be in serious trouble. And so when I saw this ad in the paper I thought this might be the end of my problems. They are so very plausible. They say: just sign this paper and then you will have no worries at all. We can get you out of it. You will be far better off if you do what we say. You can buy back whatever you need at a price you can afford and then we will make some arrangement for you in the Isle of Man. Don't worry, it's all perfectly legal.'

Porter now bitterly regrets what he did: for some months he was too ashamed to admit, even to his solicitor, that he had simply picked the firm out of a newspaper. But as his attractive Dutch wife said: 'We had had the business for fifteen years. And we didn't start it to close it down. We wanted it to be a success. But they play on your feelings: boy, how they can talk. You are very muddled and don't think straight.'

Shortly after Christmas Porter had a visit from a man called Wallace Kennedy who seemed extremely helpful. 'He was a very regular guy: he didn't smoke or drink and seemed very fond of children,' said Porter. Kennedy gave the business a quick once-over and a week later called to say that he would like Porter to drive up to Birmingham to meet a friend who might be able to help, a certain John Corscadden.

Bearded and with a taste for full-length leather greatcoats of the type worn by the German High Command during the war, Corscadden boasts an impressive string of twenty-four letters after his name. But an investigation by the BBC's Watchdog programme in the summer of 1983 revealed that he is not entitled to at least nine of them. Nonetheless Corscadden carries on a thriving business as a company liquidator. He has a large house in Altrincham, a prosperous Manchester suburb, and drives expensive foreign cars. Volvos and Peugeots are preferred.

A short inspection of Porter's business was all that was needed for Corscadden to conclude that the business should be wound up there and then. He persuaded Porter to put the company into what is known as a 'creditors' voluntary liquidation', this being one of the commonest and easiest methods of the winding-up process. The directors merely put to the shareholders a resolution proposing that the company should be wound up. But as usually only the directors are present this is often no more than a formality. At this stage the creditors do not get a look in; they are neither present nor consulted. It is a move which automatically leads to the appointment with full powers of a provisional liquidator. The directors are given so much discretion that once the liquidator has gained the confidence of the board he is more than half-way there. 'Getting the chairman's ear', as it is known in the trade, is the name of the game. Not only does it ensure that he gets his foot in the door but if his appointment is challenged when the creditors' meeting is eventually called the chairman's support and his control of the all-important proxy votes will often be enough to defeat the opposition.

In theory the liquidator is not supposed to have such a free hand. Under Section 293 of the 1948 Companies Act a creditors' meeting should be held within twenty-four hours of the shareholders' meeting to examine the statement of affairs, to appoint a committee of inspection and to confirm the appointment of the liquidator. Failure to do so carries a penalty of £100. But in practice this rarely happens, thanks to a technique called 'Centrebinding'. Its origins are respectable but it has been manipulated by the cowboys to their own advantage. 'It is a bit like aspirin in that it has probably killed as many as it was meant to cure,' said its inventor, Bernard Phillips.

THE JOY OF CENTREBINDING

It is a practice that takes its name from an obscure Essex printing company which went into liquidation in 1966, hotly pursued by the Inland Revenue which was threatening to put in the bailiffs to seize vital machinery. The liquidator was Bernard Phillips, now a senior partner with Arthur Andersen. Quiet-spoken and immaculately groomed he is one of the best-known liquidators in the business. 'If the Revenue had had their way, the company would have closed down there and then: the Revenue would have got their money but there would have been nothing left for anyone else,' he said. The problem was that as preferred creditors the Revenue was first in line. If the Revenue could jump in before the shareholders' and creditors' meetings had been held there was nothing to stop it seizing the machinery. To help save the assets on which the life of the company depended Phillips therefore needed to bring forward the share-holders' meeting and immediately put the company into liquidation. This he did. A fortnight later he held the creditors' meeting and his appointment was ratified by the creditors. This then had the desired effect of placing the machinery beyond the reach of the Revenue. The Revenue was furious and took Phillips to court. But the judgement in *R. v. Centrebinding* was in Phillips's favour. The judge concluded that although Phillips had not followed the regulations which required that the creditors' meeting should be held within twenty-four hours, nevertheless what he had done was in the best interests of the creditors. In this fashion a door was opened through which less scrupulous operators were later to rush. 'What often happens now,' says Phillips ruefully, 'is that the cowboys get the shareholders to wind up the company, delay the creditors' meeting indefinitely and in the meantime flog off all the assets to their chums.'

Once installed in Roger Porter's company, West Ferry Garages, John Corscadden quickly got down to business. The petrol company called to drain the tanks and the five company cars and a ramp were sold back to Porter at, he says, about 50 per cent below their market value. There was some discussion with his partner about the ethics of this but Porter said: 'Why not? If we don't buy them somebody else will and then nobody will be better off.' He was, however, worried about the creditors' meeting. Corscadden brushed this aside. 'We don't need to have one, and I don't want one,' he said. 'Don't worry. I'm Centre-binding.'

The result was that although the shareholders put the company into liquidation in January 1983, no creditors' meeting was held until the following April. And though little was seen of Corscadden in the following four months some £12,000 of the company's assets were sold off. Much of the stock, Porter says, disappeared and was never properly accounted for. Porter eventually became so uneasy that he asked his bank manager to find another liquidator to present to the creditors' meeting which was eventually called by Corscadden at an hotel in Swiss Cottage. The professionals who had had their eye on Corscadden turned out in force. It proved to be a very noisy affair. 'I have never seen anything like it,' said Porter. After a good deal of shouting and arm-waving Corscadden was thrown out and the new liquidator began a long and expensive legal action to recover the money.

Corscadden may in the end have lost the job but the use of the Centrebinding technique had given him the run of West Ferry Garages, uninterrupted and unsupervised, for a good four months.

HOW TO PLAY THE PROXY GAME

It is a game that everybody plays; not just the cowboys. And its object is quite simple: to influence or manipulate the creditors' meeting in your favour.

Effective as it is, even the Centrebinding technique cannot delay a creditors' meeting indefinitely. At most it creates a space of three or four months in which to work. But often more time is needed. As we have already seen, once a liquidator is in situ it takes a lot of effort, and co-ordinated effort, to unseat him. The rules say that a liquidator's appointment can only be overturned by a majority of creditors by number and value. In other words, even if a numerical majority of creditors vote against him, if the liquidator has even one very large creditor on his side, he can still keep the job – which is why the cowboys play the proxy game so vigorously.

In this scenario the company chairman plays an all-important role. Strange as it might seem the creditors' meeting is almost invariably chaired not by a creditor but by the chairman of the insolvent company who is, more often than not, committed to the acting liquidator as it was he who installed him in the first place. But getting the chairman on your side is only the first stage in the game. For the bent liquidator the job now is to consolidate this advantage by manipulating the proxies in such a way as to override the wishes of the creditors. The rules governing proxies are so complex and so little understood that this is easily done. The law lays down that every creditor must fill in a proxy form nominating whom he wishes to act for him at the creditors' meeting. Many, through ignorance or inertia, give their votes to the chairman, his being the only name they recognise. Others, thinking wrongly but not unreasonably that proxies are only for those who do not intend to go to the meeting, do not bother to fill them in; only to discover to their surprise that they have no vote at all. And thus the chairman's faction carries the day and the rogue liquidator gets the job.

Sometimes even more dubious stratagems are needed. The BBC's Watchdog programme recently investigated the collapse in December 1982 of a Manchester restaurant, owing a total of £160,000, or so it seemed. But close inquiry revealed that many of the debts were either wholly fictitious or had been deliberately inflated. It appeared that the object of the exercise was to ensure that the appointment of the acting liquidator, our old friend John Corscadden, would go through smoothly at the creditors' meeting. For if it could be shown that 'his' creditors were owed more than the others, then his position could not be legally challenged. In the event the outraged creditors put up a vigorous fight and brought in the Official Receiver to take over from Corscadden.

The simplest and commonest technique of all is to hold the creditors' meeting but to have it at such an inconvenient place and time that no one bothers to attend. 'What these boys are counting on is the basic apathy of your average creditor,' said Spicer and Pegler's Richard Turton. Thus a surprising number of Midland companies, for example, have met their ends late on a Friday afternoon in the smart but unfamiliar surroundings of some South Coast resort hotel.

THE CASE OF THE VANISHING ORGANS

Maurice Sidney Caplan has in his time employed most of these devices. He was one of the pioneers of Centrebinding and you have to move fast to catch him at a creditors' meeting. But to see Hissing Sid at his most ingenious we need to look at the case of the vanishing organs.

The story starts in 1981 when a charming Indian entrepreneur from Manchester called Amrik Singh Luther ran into difficulties. For some years previously Luther had been selling, through a company called Chase Consultants Ltd with shops in Manchester, Leicester and London, a whole range of synthesisers, organs, guitars and other musical equipment. His prices were highly competitive and the business grew fast. At the height of his fortunes he had a turnover of more than £1 million. But because of opposition from his competitors he was prevented, so Luther claims, from acting for the major manufacturers like Yamaha and so remained on the margins. In 1979, in an attempt to break into the big time, Luther travelled to the States and signed up with an American company in Boston, ARP Synthesisers, to become its British distributor. And although a new company, Chase Musicians Ltd, was set up for this purpose, in practice a lot of the business was handled by the original company, Chase Consultants Ltd, which, to make the confusion worse, actually traded as Chase Musicians. Quite properly, however, separate accounts were kept for the two limited companies. An understanding of this set-up is important as it is the key to one of Hissing Sid's most inventive frauds.

His opportunity came in the spring of 1982. The deal with the Boston synthesiser company had come unstuck as ARP had itself gone bust the previous year, leaving Chase Musicians Ltd high and dry. In an attempt to drum up new business for Musicians Ltd Luther went deeper into the organ business and borrowed £50,000 from his other company, Consultants Ltd, to purchase stock. One of his first deals was to buy for £9000 on a sale-and-return basis a consignment of organs from a company called Trevor Daniels which was based in Milton Keynes and run by the brother of Paul Daniels, the TV magician. But shortly after this deal was struck Trevor Daniels also collapsed and Hissing Sid was appointed as the liquidator. Shortly thereafter Luther was presented by Sid's agent, a debt-collecting firm called Securadebt, with a bill for £16,935. A lively argument then followed in the course of which the agent said:

'What's the matter? Are you hard up or something?'

'Who isn't?' Luther replied.

'In that case, I think I know somebody who can help you. His name is Caplan and he's as hot as mustard.'

In the insolvency world the name was well known, but to Luther it meant nothing. So he agreed to see him and about a week later Hissing Sid himself paid a call.

To Luther's surprise Sid showed little interest in his disputed debt to Trevor Daniels. He asked to see Luther's books and after a quick examination made a suggestion that so alarmed Luther, a part-time lay preacher to the Sikh community, that he went hurrying round to the Manchester Fraud Squad. The police already knew all about Hissing Sid: they had been trying to catch him at work for years. But initially they were suspicious of Luther himself and subjected him to a severe grilling. Only after he had satisfied them that he was an honest man did the police move in and set up a trap for Sid.

Going Bust

The planning was elaborate and meticulous. Luther's small office in Oldham Street, Manchester, was wired for sound. One tape recorder was strapped to Luther's thigh with the microphone concealed in his long, black beard, there was another back-up recorder hidden in the desk and in an adjoining room there was a transmitter which would send every word of the conversation to police headquarters a couple of miles away. Luther was told before the interview started to draw back the blinds of his office windows so that the police, stationed in a van across the street, could film the entire proceedings.

The police were careful not to tell Luther who Hissing Sid was for they feared that if he had realised he was entertaining one of Britain's most notorious cowboy liquidators he would take fright and refuse to co-operate. For the police it was an opportunity not to be missed. Normally they are obliged painfully to reconstruct events long after they have happened. In this case they were being given a ringside seat.

With everything in place another meeting between Luther and Caplan was arranged for the morning of May 19, 1982. Caplan was late and by the time he arrived, shortly after one o'clock, nerves were as tight as piano wire.

No sooner had Caplan arrived than the tape recorders began to roll. The conversation started with routine pleasantries. And once these were out of the way, the two men discussed the £16,000 that Luther supposedly owed Trevor Daniels for the organs. But this was no more than a preliminary to Caplan's real purpose: to stage-manage a bankruptcy of Luther's mini-empire in such a way that Luther and, of course, Caplan, would emerge unscathed. The only people to suffer would be the unfortunate and unsuspecting creditors. Throughout the three-hour conversation Luther, who is a qualified cost and management accountant, played the part of the dumb innocent.

'So who loses out? Somebody must lose out if I gain?' he asked at one stage.

'Creditors,' Caplan replied.

'Sorry?'

'Creditors,' Caplan repeated, finding it hard to believe that somebody could be so naive. 'The Crown doesn't lose, the bank doesn't lose. The creditors do. And the person who gains is you, who buys it all back.'

What Caplan had spotted was that by chance Luther's companies provided a near-perfect vehicle for a copybook fraud. Of the two companies in question, Chase Consultants Ltd and Chase Musicians Ltd, it was the latter that was in real trouble: as its debts exceeded its assets by some £46,000 it was in fact teetering on the verge of insolvency. Chase Consultants Ltd, on the other hand, was reasonably healthy with a positive balance of some £70,000. Taken together the entire group was just about solvent, though the situation was deteriorating fast. It did not take Caplan long to spot the opportunity. Because the two companies had such similar names (Chase Consultants Ltd, remember, was trading as Chase Musicians even though it was a separate entity from Chase Musicians Ltd), the invoices from suppliers were often so unclear that it was next to impossible for an outsider to tell what belonged to which company. The only man who could sort it all out was Luther himself who balanced the books at the end of each month. This was the situation that Caplan set out to exploit.

The plan was simplicity itself. What Caplan proposed was a straightforward swap of assets and liabilities between the two companies: thus the bulk of all Chase Musicians' liabilities (the ambiguous invoices and the £50,000 loan to be described as a fictitious 'management fee') would be transferred to the Chase Consultants' balance sheet, while the majority of the stock and other assets would be switched from Consultants Ltd to Musicians Ltd. The effect of this manoeuvre would be both dramatic and immediate. Overnight, Musicians Ltd would be transformed from being a very sick company into a healthy one and Consultants Ltd, now denuded of assets and loaded with liabilities, would be an instant candidate for liquidation — courtesy of Hissing Sid.

The company would not be stripped entirely bare: there would be enough money to pay off the bank and the preferred creditors, but there would of course be nothing left for the ordinary unsecured. Sid suggested that once Consultants Ltd had been put into liquidation he would arrange for those assets that had not already been transferred to Musicians Ltd to be sold back to Luther at a knock-down price.

In this fashion, Sid suggested, Luther could make a profit of half a million pounds. 'Look,' he said, warming to his theme, 'you come along and do a private deal with the auctioneers, what we call a deal by private treaty. They have valued it at £100,000. You go in and offer £105,000 and they will accept it because you have offered more than the estimated value. So now, if you are sitting on say £500,000-worth of stock that cost you £100,000 or thereabouts, this is where your profit is. That's where the real money is, and you've cut out liabilities of close on £500,000.'

All that was needed to put this plan into effect was, Caplan argued, a bit of creative accounting. Leave it all to me, he said, you won't have to worry about a thing. 'The books may be perfect,' he said, 'but the actual business itself, the vehicle, has got a bit confused. And we are going to straighten it all out. We will produce a statement of affairs, then we will decide what to do; but while we are doing that we will decipher what belongs to each company and correct it.' Caplan said that he could put Luther in touch with a firm of chartered accountants who would do the job with no questions asked. 'If it costs a couple of thousand,' he said, 'it makes no bloody difference. At least you are getting the answers you want.'

So, as it turned out, were the police. Shortly afterwards Caplan was arrested and told that everything he had said had been recorded. For once the voluble Caplan was lost for words.

7 Change the Name
the Game's the Same

THE ORIGINS of limited liability in Britain go back over a hundred years – to the Companies Acts of 1856 and 1862. At the time it was a necessary reform. Companies, hungry for capital, were straining against the confines of the traditional family partnership. The increasing size and scale of business activity meant that even the richest entrepreneurs often lacked the resources to expand; and while they remained personally liable for all their debts they were understandably reluctant to try. So the concept of limited liability was introduced as a spur to enterprise: to encourage risk-taking by deliberately minimising the penalties of failure.

The effects were both immediate and dramatic. In the years between 1856 and 1883, the year of Joe Chamberlain's Bankruptcy Act, more than 20,000 entrepreneurs took advantage of the offered protection to form limited companies. And though the early years saw a good proportion of failures – the collapse of Overend and Gurney, the City bankers, which went down for £18 million in 1866 being the most famous example – the Acts encouraged a process that has continued uninterrupted to this day. The latest count shows that there are nearly 1.5 million limited companies in existence in Great Britain though perhaps only two thirds are actively trading.

But over the years limited liability has proved to be a double-edged device. While it protects the virtuous it also offers a wonderfully convenient shelter for the crooked, the unscrupulous or the merely sharp who have invented a practice known as 'Change the name the game's the same'.

It is very common, is quite legal and works like this: the company director decides that his firm should no longer continue trading and it is put into voluntary liquidation. A liquidator is appointed who takes charge and tidies up the company's affairs. The assets are sold off and the more pressing debts discharged. But very often the very same assets are sold back at knock-down prices to the original owner who then simply changes the name of the company and opens up again, sometimes the very next day. The dismayed creditors are left to contemplate the wreckage. They rarely obtain much, if any, satisfaction for reasons which I hope will become clear. But the architect of this little manoeuvre need not lose a penny of his own money. He is free to walk away from the crash quite unscathed – thanks to limited liability.

I had been told that members of the garment business were among the most artful of these dodgers so I went to see Keith Goodman, a senior partner of Leonard Curtis & Co, who are known in the insolvency business as specialists in the rag trade. Goodman, whose own family were once East End tailors, began by explaining why the trade appeared to be so accident-prone.

It is, he explained, no longer a Jewish monopoly: most of the small manufacturers these days are Pakistanis or Greek Cypriots. But the basic characteristics have not changed. It is still, as it was eighty years ago, based on outworkers who take parcels of cloth from the manufacturers, cut out the pieces around the paper patterns provided and then make up the suits or dresses – a business known in the trade as 'cut, make and trim'. As employers, the outworkers are, of course, liable for PAYE and VAT but as they are invariably little people running small companies and working on very tight margins they rarely bother to build these into their costings. Suddenly, Goodman says, they are faced with a huge tax bill. So what do they do? They go and see their accountant who says: 'OK, you have a limited company. You have no creditors except the Revenue but you do have a factory full of goods and machinery. So why not wind up the company and then buy back the lease and the stock from the liquidator? Nobody is going to object: the Revenue never attend creditors' meetings so there will be no hostile creditors to make a fuss. And as you will be the only buyer the liquidator will have to sell your stuff back to you.' Very often, Goodman says, the banks will actually lend the owner the money for the purpose. 'It's all very simple: overnight they are back on the treadmill until it happens all over again. I know of companies who have done this not once or twice but many times. And the only people who lose out are the Revenue and the VATman. Most of them are not crooks. They don't actually want to go into liquidation. It is just that as the law stands it is the easiest way out of their difficulties.'

This is a very simple if widely practised example of the game. To see it raised to the status of an art-form we must study the careers of two London-based entrepreneurs, Barry Freeman and Sydney Newman. The numerous collapses of their various and multi-titled businesses owed little or nothing either to the demands of the taxman or to the vagaries of business life. Throughout they appeared to have taken maximum advantage of the kindly laws of limited liability and to have rung the changes in a series of ingenious permutations in such a way that when their companies went bust the cupboard was usually bare. So let us look first at the life and times of Barry Freeman.

A man of stocky build and medium height in his mid-forties, he had a taste for stylish clothes and gold jewellery; he was rarely seen without his bracelet and chest medallion. In the early eighties he lived in a comfortable house in Edgware, a prosperous North London suburb, his wife drove a sports car, he drove a Rolls and his children went to private school. He liked to keep his overheads to a minimum. As a businessman he rarely bought anything for cash: he preferred rented premises, vehicles on hire purchase, self-employed staff working on commission, heavy advertising on credit and a share capital which did not exceed the legal minimum of two £1 shares. His real skill was not making but selling – and very often the main property he was marketing was himself. His customers invariably described him as a smooth and convincing talker.

By the time Freeman enters our story in the autumn of 1980 he had already had a long and apparently profitable history of failure behind him. Three of his companies had either gone or were in the process of going bust. The last was a home improvement concern called Henley Properties which when last heard of was trading as Tempo Windows from rented premises in a Victorian block at 653/659 Commercial Road in the East End of London. For months before it was put into the hands of the Official Receiver, on October 13, 1980, there had been angry complaints from customers as far away as Poole in Dorset, pressing for deposits to be repaid or work completed. So great was the clamour that the Office of Fair Trading began to take a lively interest. And when in November 1981 the Official Receiver finally completed his inquiry into the affairs of Henley Properties he discovered that there were next to no assets to cover debts of more than £100,000.

If anybody was responsible for this lamentable state of affairs it was not, so the record seemed to show, Barry Freeman as he was not even listed as a director of the company: his wife Caryl fulfilled that role. Freeman himself appeared merely as company secretary. There was, however, no doubt as to who was actually in charge. To customers Freeman regularly described himself as managing director and when in the course of time the Office of Fair Trading demanded a legal assurance that the directors of Henley Properties would trade fairly in future it was Freeman himself who signed the document.

But by this time Freeman had lost interest in home improvements: video games were the latest craze. And so Freeman created a new enterprise with the hopeful title of Cash Flow Investment Services (CFIS) which was born on November 1, 1980, only seventeen days after the legal death of Henley Properties and which, curiously, shared the same address.

The idea behind CFIS was to cash in on the arcade boom by leasing the machines on a franchise basis to investors; the machines would be sited in such 'tested' money-making locations as hamburger stores, fish-and-chip shops, mini-cab offices and clubs.

But to complete the jigsaw one further piece was needed. This was provided by a £100 off-the-shelf company called Jobed Ltd which had been incorporated as a limited company some weeks before CFIS actually started trading. As CFIS was merely a trading name, it was Jobed Ltd, the company, which was supplying the all-important protection of its limited liability status.

The man Freeman chose to help him run Jobed had a career at least as chequered as his own. Alfred Leon Ostroff was a roly-poly man with thinning, slicked-back hair, bulging eyes and a bizarre sense of humour. When a black customer later visited the offices of Jobed to make a complaint, Ostroff dropped on one knee and offered him his version of the Al Jolson classic 'Mammy'. Throughout the sixties and seventies Ostroff and his partner Alan Lipman ran companies offering a whole range of services – from central heating to deep freeze. The only common characteristic was that they appeared to be remarkably short-lived. Five were dissolved by the Registrar of Companies, three became insolvent and went into liquidation with Ostroff's own accountant appointed as liquidator, and one was compulsorily wound up after a client complained that he had paid £8000 for a flat in Spain which he never received.

Now they had found a new game to play. The key to the operation was a heavy advertising campaign in such papers as the *Daily Express*, *Exchange & Mart* and the *London Weekly Advertiser*. The promises seemed – and were – too good to be true. 'Beat inflation,' said the advertisements. 'Extra income between £60 and £100 net can easily be made per week . . . We specialise in giving tremendous, successful, proven business opportunities to individuals in the multi-million space-age leisure industry.' For this 'tremendous' opportunity customers paid as much as £1400 with 45 per cent of the takings going to the franchisee, 45 per cent to the owner of the site and a modest 10 per cent to Barry Freeman's companies.

The advertising campaign attracted hundreds of hopeful investors. It was supported by a team of salesmen working on commission who distributed glossy leaflets giving the impression that the machines were brand new and made at CFIS's own factory in Lancashire. This was not true. Nearly all the machines were second-hand and in poor condition. Far from being worth anything like the £1400 some of the punters were being asked to pay, respectable manufacturers valued them at no more than

£150 apiece. Deliveries were also erratic. Many customers were still waiting for delivery six months after posting their cheques. One customer from Rainham in Essex who had invested his redundancy money in the project was paying CFIS a regular £25.75 a month by standing order, but months after the payments started he still had no machine. Some machines broke down, were removed for repair and then never reappeared; others lacking serial numbers or clear identification led to angry disputes over title when missing machines mysteriously turned up elsewhere. And when irate customers turned up at the offices to press their claims, Freeman and his colleagues proved to be highly elusive.

But despite delays and complaints the money rolled in: altogether CFIS collected over £100,000. In December 1980 the parent company, Jobed Ltd, even succeeded in acquiring a licence, issued in Freeman's name, from the Office of Fair Trading enabling it to offer hire purchase terms to its customers at the very time when the previous Freeman operation, Henley Properties, was being investigated by the selfsame body for improper trading.

Even so, as the publicity CFIS's shortcomings attracted was becoming bad for business, Freeman decided to take evasive action. Together with Ostroff he revived a dormant company, Stargrange Ltd, which had been set up in 1977, offering an identical video game deal to that advertised by CFIS. Customers may have thought it was an entirely separate enterprise but in fact it was the very same operation under another name.

It was, however, only a rearguard action. Time was clearly running out for CFIS which is why some months later a new set of characters – and some not so new – appeared on the stage.

In the summer of 1981 a flame-haired, shapely divorcee from the Isle of Man called Brenda Lowe, a former CFIS sales rep and a close friend of Barry Freeman's, rented a one-room office above a Wimpy bar on London's Clapham Common. She too was selling video games through a business called BB Commercial Enterprises. But as Mrs Lowe was then an undischarged bankrupt the business was registered in the name of her twenty-one-year-old son Jeremy and a certain Clive James who gave his address as the Isle of Man. In fact 'Mr James' was none other than Barry Freeman in disguise. In short order the business was remodelled. It was re-registered with two new partners, Mrs Lowe's eighty-year-old mother Lila Gold and Barry Freeman himself who now emerged under his true colours. The business shifted its address from Clapham Junction to the one used by Stargrange in Shoreditch and opened up for business. Later some customers were to find that their machines were identical in type to those supplied by CFIS. Readers of such publications as the *London Weekly Advertiser*, which had banned the CFIS ads after a barrage of complaints, were told: 'The only thing better than making money is making MORE money.'

By November 1981 the new-born enterprise was in full swing as were, strangely enough, the proceedings to close down the now discredited CFIS/Jobed/Stargrange operation.

Later that month Freeman told the BBC's Checkpoint programme, which had been following his affairs with close attention, that Jobed Ltd was to go into voluntary liquidation. Its debts amounted to £132,000 of which £60,000 was owing to the investors, one of whom was so angry that he picketed Freeman's home.

A creditors' meeting was duly summoned for December 14, 1981, but as none of the directors put in an appearance the company was left in limbo. It was only after a group of investors, encouraged by the staff of the consumer advice centre at the London Borough of Tower Hamlets, had chipped in £5 apiece that enough money was raised to petition the courts for a compulsory winding-up order. This was eventually granted. Its affairs therefore passed into the hands of the Official Receiver who on February 7, 1983, more than a year later, reported that the company's assets fell far short of its liabilities. Furthermore Barry Freeman had been spared the bother and expense of putting the company into liquidation himself: the entire costs of the winding-up exercise had fallen on the creditors and the taxpayer.

In the case of Stargrange, Freeman ignored even these bare formalities. The operations were simply closed down and the staff transferred to BB Commercial Enterprises, which operated out of the old Stargrange office in Shoreditch but under its new name. The manoeuvre was so successful that the landlord to whom the vanishing Stargrange owed rent did not realise that his new tenants were one and the same. Customers had a similar problem with Barry Freeman himself. On one occasion one customer who knew him as Barry Freeman and one who knew him as Clive James found themselves talking to him at the same time: they departed scratching their heads.

Very soon BBCE was operating on much the same scale as CFIS before it: and giving rise to much the same complaints. There is some evidence to suggest that shortly before the Jobed collapse Freeman arranged to put some of its assets beyond the reach of the bailiffs by switching them to the new company, BBCE. Freeman tried to distance himself by hiding behind Brenda Lowe but in fact he was, as always, the puppet master.

By April 1982, less than five months after the secret face-lift, BBCE suffered the same fate as its predecessors. The company was abandoned leaving the creditors to whistle for their money. However morally questionable it may be, it is perfectly legal for a director to leave his company in limbo – neither trading nor in liquidation. It can merely cease to trade and leave the creditors to petition the court to wind it up if they wish. As BBCE was never formally put in liquidation it is impossible to gauge its debts at the time of the collapse. All that one can say is that neither Barry Freeman nor his friends lost money. It was the customers who paid the price. Several bought as many as ten machines for sums up to £11,000. One man from Guildford parted with £15,000 for fifteen machines and months later he was still trying to lay his hands on the machines and the keys for the cash boxes. Sadly, after a prolonged court battle with Freeman, he committed suicide in 1983.

But by this time the ever-nimble Freeman was long gone. He had found yet another game to play, though the rules remained much the same as before. The chosen vehicle was three companies called Photo-Fast (UK) Ltd, Gilmartin Property Company Ltd (trading as the official sounding Grants and Building Advisory Service) and, confusingly, BB Commercial Enterprises Ltd, which, though it had almost exactly the same name as the now dying video game company, had popped up again under a new guise. The key difference between the old BB and the new was that the former was a partnership while the latter was a limited company, which in theory should have given Freeman some measure of protection.

Thus Freeman entered the third phase of his remarkable career. With the faithful Brenda Lowe at his side, Photo-Fast (UK) Ltd was set up to offer another 'amazing' investment opportunity. The scheme this time involved a machine that printed photographs on plates and for which investors were invited to lay down £5000 which would, so the advertisement claimed, net them a truly incredible £1500 profit a week. 'Once you have seen it – your mind will boggle,' investors were told. The *Daily Express*, which carried these ads, was less impressed. In November 1982 the paper went to court to have the company wound up. One down and two to go. But there we must leave Barry Freeman and turn our attention to another operator, just as brazen and just as ingenious: Sydney Newman.

In July 1980 the 20,000 owners of a small, domestic dishwasher called the Lylybet received a disturbing letter. It informed them that the firm which had made and serviced the appliance had unfortunately gone into liquidation and that they were no longer covered by the manufacturer's guarantee. If they wished for a continuing supply of spare parts, the letter went on, would they kindly send £11.50 to a company calling itself Dishmaster (Home Counties) Ltd. What the letter did not mention, however, was that the firm, which had gone bust owing nearly £250,000, was run by the very same man who was now apparently offering a way out of the difficulty. Nor did the circular explain how it was that the helpful Dishmaster (Home Counties) Ltd had come by the spares in the first place. We will return to Lylybet later but first we must introduce the author of the circular.

Sydney Newman, like Barry Freeman, is a fast-moving North London entrepreneur. For the past ten years he had had an unrivalled record of failure in two separate fields, domestic appliances and home improvements (see Appendix Two). His companies tended to be family concerns. His co-director was invariably Eunice Roberta Newman, the wife of his son Maurice. Maurice's business career does not appear to have been blessed with success either.

Throughout the 1960s Maurice Newman ran a string of building and home improvement businesses in Essex and London, all of which appear to have fallen on hard times. In 1970 Maurice was adjudged bankrupt and was therefore debarred from taking an active part in the family's business affairs until his discharge in 1980. But just before Maurice's bankruptcy yet another home improvement company, Loft Rooms (London), sprang into being. Its directors were Maurice's wife Eunice and his father Sydney.

The company traded, apparently successfully, for some eight years. In the last twenty months of its life it had a turnover of over £600,000. But in December 1978 it ceased its activities. And when Loft Rooms (London) eventually went into voluntary liquidation two and a half years later its assets were reported to be no more than £41.

But that was not the end of the Newmans' interest in the home improvement business: far from it. Eleven months before shutting down Loft Rooms (London) Ltd the Newmans had started another company called Loft Rooms (Southern) Ltd, whose name was later changed to simply Loft Rooms Ltd. It was not long before this company too was in difficulties. By 1979 it was reporting a loss of over £65,000 on a reported turnover of more than £500,000. In addition the creditors were owed £130,000. But Sydney Newman was not deterred: he was busy expanding the other side of his small empire – the Lylybet dishwasher business.

From about 1969 onwards he had been operating simultaneously as a specialist in home conversions and as a purveyor of a small, Italian-designed, counter-top dishwasher called the Lylybet. Its main selling point was that the Lylybet, like John Bloom's more famous machine, needed no plumbing and could immediately be hooked up to the kitchen taps.

This business too was to have a chequered history. Between

1970 and 1978 no fewer than five dishwasher companies were either wound up or went into liquidation. And in each case the pattern was the same: lots of debts and very few assets. There may not seem to be much in common between automatic dishwashers and domestic lofts but what linked these disparate enterprises was their habit of disappearing only to reappear shortly afterwards in a new form, leaving behind a trail of unsettled debts and dissatisfied customers. As one of his many creditors put it: 'Newman is a survivor. His companies don't survive but he certainly does.' In this respect Sydney lived up to his own name: he was a new man again and again and again.

Newman's own appearances were a good deal less frequent than those of his companies. For inquiring journalists he was an elusive quarry. When once caught on the telephone he said he would only answer questions in writing. 'Could I have an interview?' the journalist inquired. 'That's a question,' Newman replied and put down the phone. And when written questions were submitted there was no reply.

There is, of course, no law which prevents a man setting up as many companies as he likes in the legitimate pursuit of his business. Nor is it necessarily illegal to spread one's liabilities between them so that when one collapses it is still possible to keep going with the others: it is a practice regularly recommended by the most respectable of accountants. But Sydney Newman appears to have carried this technique to extremes. And it is best illustrated by the history of the Lylybet dishwasher.

When Newman acquired the Lylybet franchise, after flirting with other machines, he appeared to be on to a good thing. He took over the manufacture from the Italians and retailed the machine at around £250. It was heavily promoted in the national press as 'the dishwasher with a difference' and by 1977 the company, Lylybet Dishwashers (UK) Ltd, had a turnover of around £250,000 of which some 40 per cent was export. For a small private company the profits were reasonable.

But by 1978 the company was in trouble. The balance sheet moved into the red and the liabilities began, as so often before, to mount. There were complaints to the Advertising Standards Authority and in two cases these were upheld.

The company held out for another couple of years. But in June 1980 Newman approached the well-known insolvency firm of Bernard Phillips & Co (now amalgamated with Arthur Andersen) and asked to be put into liquidation. A statement of affairs prepared by the accountants for the creditors' meeting revealed that there was a deficiency of £192,705. Preferential creditors who included the Inland Revenue were owed nearly £60,000 and ninety-eight unsecured creditors had claims totalling £143,280. Assets such as plant, equipment, furniture and stock had a book value totalling £160,000 but the liquidator estimated that if they were put up for sale they would realise no more than £17,600.

Even this proved to be optimistic. When the final accounts were published it transpired that the assets had in fact only fetched £3400 and that the only viable purchaser was Sydney Newman himself. Furthermore he had cleverly retained a copy of the entire list of his 20,000 customers. He was therefore in an excellent position to start all over again. On July 14, 1980, just four days after his creditors heard the news of the collapse of the Lylybet company, Newman put the list to use. He wrote to his former customers as Dishmaster (Home Counties) Ltd, suggesting that they might like some spares. So great was the response that a year later the new company could declare a profit of £30,000 after providing Sydney Newman and his daughter-in-law Eunice with £12,360 in directors' fees.

This was only the first stage. Very soon customers received another letter telling them that Dishmaster (Home Counties) Ltd was not just selling spares: it was making the dishwashers as well. Despite unpaid debts of £192,000 Newman was back in business. He had bought back his plant, and retained the much-advertised trading name and the all-important list of customers. And when, just a month after the collapse, the name was changed to Dishmaster (Lylybet) Ltd the transformation was complete. The old sales brochures for which Newman had never paid were simply recycled after the old trading address at the bottom had been snipped off. Newman celebrated this coup by buying himself a new Mercedes. Change the name, the game's the same.

*

So how, it may be asked, do operators like Newman and Freeman get away with it? There are many reasons.

First, they benefit from the protection of the laws of limited liability which are now widely recognised as being in urgent need of reform. The professionals in the insolvency business tend to be cynical, hard-headed men with a strong vested interest in the status quo. But almost everyone I met agreed that the situation was now out of hand. 'Limited liability provides far too much protection for the director of a failed company and far too little for the customers and the workforce. It is a national scandal,' says Bernard Phillips, who has been in the business nearly fifty years. Sir Kenneth Cork, the author of the Cork Report, is equally critical. 'The protection given by limited liability is now far too wide, with the result that people can now get away with murder,' he told me. His report says that the law is 'too indulgent of the director who emerges from the wreckage of one company and trades immediately under the protection of another limited company.'

Second, liquidators have strictly limited responsibilities. Their job is to work not for the customers or the workforce but for the creditors. And so they often concentrate on realising those assets on which they can readily lay their hands rather than mounting a long, detailed investigation into the company's affairs at their own expense.

Third, the system is biased in favour of small company directors, especially those who succeed in salting away the assets prior to the crash. The private liquidators are in the business for profit and earn their money by charging a hefty percentage on assets realised. They will often refuse to handle the smaller cases which are precisely those where, as we have seen, the abuses are most flagrant. In late 1983 I went to a creditors' meeting in Birmingham. The company in question was tiny. But because word had gone around that there might be dirty work afoot several of the big accounting firms had sent representatives. Shortly before the meeting started the professionals met in the hotel lobby to compare notes. 'Do you know if there are any assets in it?' inquired the young man from Cork Gully who had come up from London on the afternoon train. 'I do hope so, because if I go back and tell them there's nothing in it, they will kick my backside.' He went on to explain that he was leaving the firm shortly to take up a plum appointment in New York and Curaçao. 'It was an offer I just couldn't refuse,' he explained. His senior colleagues congratulated him on his new job but gently reproved him, perhaps for my benefit, for his unduly mercenary approach. 'You have to take the rough with the smooth, old son,' he was told. 'The important thing is to get the job done properly.'

Fourth, both the Official Receiver and the Fraud Squad are short of resources and badly over-worked. And the Department of Trade and Industry which has its own company investigation division frequently fobs off complaints, so the police allege, by referring them to part-time and toothless committees of inspection.

Fifth, company law allows a private company to be set up with a nominal £2 share capital so the director is not even put to the expense of a substantial personal shareholding.

Sixth, those provisions of the 1976 Insolvency Act, introduced specifically to stamp out the abuses I have described, are rarely, if ever, enforced. In theory any director whose companies have been wound up twice within five years lays himself open to a criminal prosecution for fraud. But for the action to succeed the Crown must demonstrate intent to defraud which in practice is very difficult. This section of the Act is in effect a dead letter; over the past seven years the number of successful prosecutions can be counted on the fingers of one hand. And even then the missing money is rarely recovered as the creditors have to meet the cost of the ensuing civil action out of their own pockets. Understandably, most creditors are highly reluctant to throw good money after bad.

Sir Kenneth Cork believes that changing the law is not the

answer. 'There is no point in messing about with something that will never be enforced,' he says. 'The answer is to hit the bent director where it hurts most: in his pocket.' Sir Kenneth therefore proposes that any director whose company goes bust twice within five years should be banned from setting up a limited company and thus deprived of the protection of limited liability. It is for just these people, he argues, that the full rigour of the bankruptcy law should be reserved. The Government, in designing its new legislation, has unfortunately rejected this approach as being too radical. It suggests instead that directors found guilty of what is described as 'wrongful trading' should be personally liable for the company's debts. But the definition of the offence is presently so vague as to be no real deterrent.*

Seventh, circumstances favour the sharp trader. Men like Freeman and Newman rely on the fact that no customer, supplier, policeman or official will have the full picture of their activities which take place at different times, in different places and under various disguises. Liaison between the regional fraud squads is sometimes not as close as it should be nor are relations between the police and the company investigators at the DTI particularly good. So there are many holes in the enforcement net through which a determined operator can slip.

Above all, what aids these quick-change artists is the apathy of most creditors and the widespread ignorance of the complexities of company law. Often, all directors have to do is to issue an official sounding statement that the company has ceased to trade for creditors to believe that the official machine has taken over and will safeguard their interests. The banks, secure in the knowledge that their money at least is usually safe, rarely make a fuss or even bother to attend creditors' meetings. To ordinary customers the finely calculated distinctions between one company name and another are meaningless. As long as the face in the showroom or the voice on the telephone remains the same, they tend to assume that all is well. And when the company to which they have entrusted their money goes into liquidation they are at first amazed and then outraged to discover they will never get their money back.

*For a more detailed critique of the new legislation see Postscript.

8 The Listening Banks

IT IS ONLY over the past five years or so, as Britain plunged into the deepest recession since the thirties, that the banks have begun to exercise their undoubted life-and-death power over industry. At the depths of the slump in 1982 Barclays alone pulled the plug on 618 companies while the Midland was not far behind with 510. Among the casualties were Sir Freddie Laker's airline business, Stone-Platt Industries, the textile machinery makers, once the pride of Lancashire, and virtually the entire British toy industry. The reasons for the failures vary from company to company. Overseas competition, reckless over-expansion, over-borrowing and under-capitalisation, board-room feuds and poor management – all these were factors. But in every case it was the bank that delivered the final coup de grâce. And though the crisis may have been months, or even years, in the making, when the end came it arrived in a flurry of telephone calls with appalling suddenness.

Leslie Pincott, the former chairman of Stone-Platt, still vividly remembers the day when, like a naughty schoolboy summoned to the headmaster's study, he was asked to call on the general manager of the Midland Bank and told that unless he could find £15 million of new equity there and then the bank would have no option but to appoint a receiver. He failed. The receiver was appointed at midday and by two o'clock that same day he and 120 of his staff were swarming all over the Mayfair head office. But though it is the Lakers and the Stone-Platts that capture the headlines their death agonies are rarely sudden: so much of the banks' money is involved that behind the scenes great efforts are made in an attempt to save them. It is in the main the smaller firms who have borne the brunt. And though the banks have always had the power to set such machinery in motion it is only comparatively recently that it has been so rigorously exercised.

'For twenty years,' a senior official of one of the big banks told me in the winter of 1983/4, 'the banks were protected by inflation, with the result that almost any proposition put to the bank had a chance of success and – what is more – safety. Banks measured their risks by the "gone concern" assessment. In other words they would calculate how much would be left for the bank if the company went under. Up to 1979, the banks were very limited and crude in their approach. Life was very easy. And both banks and business became very slack and unprofessional. The banks thought they were doing a good job because they never lost money. In the case of a small business, if the chairman put money behind it, the banks were happy to lend.'

But as the recession deepened and companies got further into difficulties, life became a good deal more complicated. In many cases what had seemed like an eminently safe, bankable proposition started to appear very vulnerable as bank borrowings rose, orders collapsed and the cash flow dwindled to a trickle. What made the situation even more alarming was that since the 1960s, banks had moved in to become the main suppliers of finance to industry. The Bank of England statistics show that by 1982 the clearing banks were supplying 80 per cent of industry's external finance in the form of short-term or medium-term loans. With small firms the proportion was even higher: up to 90 per cent and beyond.

In the boom years of the 60s and the early 70s the banks had scrambled for this business. 'The market became so competitive,' the clearing banker said, 'that we virtually took over the debenture market. In this atmosphere, companies became greedy and borrowed more instead of raising new capital. Company treasurers whose job it was to raise money as cheaply as possible shopped around for the best rates.' Companies who had traditionally dealt with just one bank often found themselves with more than a dozen, each with its finger in a different part of the pie. When Laker Airways crashed in February 1982, there were some twenty separate banks spread over three continents involved; and even Stone-Platt Industries, the textile machinery firm, which failed six weeks later, had at one time thirteen banks on its back.

As long as the economy was moving up, nobody worried; everybody wanted a piece of the action. But the moment the down-turn came, bankers who traditionally had only looked to the company's realisable assets for their security (the 'gone concern' approach, known in less polite circles as 'pawnbroking') began to find that they needed new and unaccustomed skills. As the debts mounted, the bankers found themselves, greatly to their alarm, becoming involved in matters of which they had little knowledge or expertise. They were forced to monitor in greater and greater detail, not just the company's financial situation but how it was being run. All sorts of questions were posed: was the company in the right line of business? Should the product be changed and, if so, how? Most crucially of all: was the management up to the job? And should the chairman go?

All these are questions that bankers by training and background are not in normal circumstances disposed to ask and are even less well-equipped to answer. It would perhaps be unfair to expect the men in Leadenhall Street to second-guess the client's marketing man or production controller. But one would expect even the local branch manager in a small provincial town to ask tough questions when one of his industrial customers got into difficulties. The evidence, however, suggests otherwise. When in 1983 the Department of Trade and Industry asked the City accounting firm, Robson Rhodes, to do a study of small entrepreneurs who had sought assistance under the Government-backed Small Business Loan Guarantee scheme, the accountants were, among other things, very critical of the role played by the banks. The firm found that most bank managers, at least at local level, were unimaginative, uncritical and more interested in the security offered than in the potential viability of the business.

'Most of the lending we studied,' Robson Rhodes reported, 'had initially been approved, fundamentally on an important, but subjective, assessment of character and the apparent credentials of the proprietors, rather than on the viability and prospects of the business . . . When under pressure on their lending record we believe that many bank managers turn not towards more thorough appraisals but to more security.'

Robson Rhodes found that most bank managers let potential industrial borrowers off surprisingly lightly. The same man who might give you or me a hard time over a request for an overdraft, is portrayed in the accountants' report as being a pushover. 'The borrower,' they say, 'was not often confronted by a banker asking what evidence he had to support his claim that there was a market, what share of that market he might hope to achieve – and how; and, if those questions were resolved, to what extent the business could withstand any assumption being disproved. In the simplest sense, in these appraisals, little attention is paid to the forecast break-even level, in spite of this being in many cases ridiculously high, or, in cases where forecasts are wildly optimistic, ridiculously low.' The accountants concluded their critique of banking practice with a sentence that must ring true in the ears of many a businessman. 'If the loan is made on spuriously optimistic forecasts . . . it becomes a question of how long it takes for the lender to lose his nerve.'

The inability of local managers properly to appraise their industrial clients is one reason why the big clearers, led by Barclays and the Midland, have, for the past ten years or so, had their own 'intensive care' units, small specialist teams based at head office. Run by tough, competent men, these units were set up in the wake of the 1973/4 property and secondary banking crisis which sent shock waves through the banking community. 'It took us a bit by surprise,' says Barclay's Stan Carslake. 'We thought we knew as much about property as the property boys did but we didn't.'

Carslake is an unusual figure for a senior banker. An extrovert East Ender, with a bashed-in, prize-fighter's face, he looks and sounds as if he would be happier at the ringside than in a banker's parlour. But as head of Barclays' 'intensive care' unit he is very much at the sharp end of the business. He and his forty-man team look after those of Barclays' clients who are teetering on the edge of the precipice. These days, so the banks say, their approach to problem companies is a good deal more sophisticated than it used to be. 'Sympathy and money is not enough: very often the last thing the company needs is money,' says one senior manager. Instead the bank will commission an independent accountant's report and then move into the firm itself to monitor every detail of the company's actual operations. It will look at its system of cash control, its budget forecasts and its marketing plans and then draw its own conclusions. The next question will be: is the existing management capable of implementing the bank's plan? The bank will pass a particularly keen eye over the chairman, the chief executive and the finance director and if any of these are found wanting, then the bank will quietly suggest that they be removed. 'It is wholly reasonable,' said one clearing banker, 'that we do not support the management who got us into this trouble.' The bankers claim that they never put in their own nominees: they are, they say, very careful to let the company itself appoint its own men. But for all this smooth talk it is very clear that when companies get into trouble it is very much a case of 'he who pays the piper calls the tune'. As the banks always work behind the scenes their muscle is rarely apparent. The only real argument is at what stage this power should be deployed and for whose benefit. All too often the complaint is that bankers' power is exercised too late and then solely on behalf of the bank, so that when the crash comes the bankers escape more or less unscathed while the creditors and the shareholders are left to suffer.

When I saw Stan Carslake in early 1984 he and his staff had about 600 companies on the sick list of which, he thought, a good percentage were terminal cases. Like most other people in the insolvency business, Carslake likes to see himself more as a surgeon than an undertaker. 'I don't want to be an undertaker,' he protests. 'But you live with people who have failed and you see the penalties of failure.' He talks about companies he knows but will not name which have been only twenty minutes from liquidation when the bank moved in and which survived to tell the tale. But equally, as his prime duty is to look after the bank's money, he can be very tough and unyielding. 'It's not the bank's fault that the company gets into trouble. It gets into trouble by itself – usually because of weak management,' he says. 'There is a terrible temptation to drag down the good with the bad if you leave it too late. You can't win. If you put the receiver in too early, the directors scream, and if you put him in too late, the shareholders scream.' And Carslake defends Barclays' record by saying: 'It's improper for a respectable banker to encourage firms to trade when they are actually insolvent.'

But for all the emphasis the banks now place on 'intensive care', the power to appoint a receiver remains the ultimate weapon. And over the past 120 years the banks have so arranged affairs that, when the crash comes, it is they who will be at or very near the head of the queue. When Laker and Stone-Platt went down, it was the creditors, the customers and the employees who lost out: the banks, who had financed the expansion in the first place without asking too many questions about the viability of the enterprises, escaped comparatively lightly. This is the reason why the banks are so unpopular in this kind of situation. Financing companies, especially high fliers like Laker, is a risky business but if things go wrong, then surely, it is argued, the risks should be evenly spread.

The power of the receiver rests on a curious legal device invented by the Court of Chancery in the second half of the nineteenth century known as the floating charge. A feature of English law since the 1860s, it is unknown on the Continent and was only introduced into Scotland by statute as late as 1961. Described by one banking textbook as 'a charge which floats or hovers like a hawk over all the assets of the company as they change in the ordinary course of business' it is a truly remarkable device. It gives the lender an effective mortgage over present and future assets of the company and enables him to call in the loan at any time. The holder of a floating charge ranks behind such preferred creditors as the Inland Revenue and the VATman but ahead of all other secured and unsecured creditors. And among the conditions is the power to appoint a receiver whose job it is to collect those monies thus secured.

It is, both for the lender and the borrower, a very convenient and flexible device: it offers the bank maximum security while giving the company access to cash it might not otherwise be able to obtain – which is why the floating charge is now such a feature of English commercial life. But from the moment of its birth it has been vigorously attacked by almost everybody except the banks – by judges, accountants and, of course, other creditors. As far back as 1905 Mr Justice Buckley in *Re: London Pressed Hinge Co Ltd* commented: 'Directly the receiver is appointed, the expectation of the creditor is intercepted. He may have lent his money, or consigned his goods, to the company last week: but if he has the audacity to ask for payment and to enforce his legal remedies to obtain it, the debenture-holder obtains a receiver in a proceeding to which the execution creditor is not a party, and thus closes the door against him, taking his money and his goods as part of the security, and leaving the creditor who supplied the money or goods to go unpaid. I regret to be driven to the conclusion that, as the law stands, those are the rights of the debenture-holder entitled to a floating charge ... It is an injustice arising from the nature as defined by the authorities of a floating security. The mischief arises from the fact that the law allows a charge on all future property. The subject, however, is one which, I think, urgently requires attention.'

The judge's complaints went unheard. When, seventy-seven years later, Sir Kenneth Cork examined the question in his monumental review of the insolvency law, he found that of all the questions under review that of the floating charge remained the most contentious. 'We have,' he wrote, 'received more evidence both oral and written on this one subject from those whom we have consulted than on any other.' And echoing the comments of the learned judge three generations before, Cork said: 'The matter for wonder is that such a device should ever have been invented by a Court of Equity. It is not easy to discern on what principle the holder of a floating charge should obtain security over goods for which his money has not paid, in priority to the claim of the unpaid supplier of the goods.' Cork recommended that, irrespective of the banks' claims under the floating charge, 10 per cent of the company's assets should be set aside for the unsecured creditors in an attempt partially to redress the balance. But this proposal was greeted with horror by the banks and regarded as too radical by the Government, which chose to tinker with the insolvency laws rather than reform them.

The floating charge, however, is by no means the only weapon in the banks' armoury. In 1979 Barclays broke new ground by winning a legal case (*Seibe Gorman and Co Ltd v. Barclays Bank Ltd*) which allowed it to take out a fixed charge against a company's future book debts. This was an important breakthrough as very often the debts of an insolvent company are an important percentage of its realisable assets. It was a further extension of bankers' power and meant that for the first time they could push their way right to the front of the queue, ahead even of the Government and other preferred creditors. Barclays may have led the way, but the others quickly followed.

The banks make no apologies for their obsession with security – what they call, revealingly, 'the belt and braces approach'. They claim that they make so little money on industrial lending – about 1½ per cent on average – that they have no alternative but to reach out and grab as much as they can. 'We need all the security we can get,' says Barclays' Stan Carslake. 'The reason we went against book debts is that with a lot of companies it is the only real asset in sight. It's all very well for the creditors: they are often cushioned by a 20 per cent mark-up; and besides they usually know when something is going wrong and can, unlike the bank, get out before the crash. But there is no way we can get out without pulling the plug. We are locked in. If we have more security we lend more and if we have less we lend less: it's as simple as that.'

So much for the theory. We have listened to the money men calmly explaining what they do and why – and all very reasonable it sounds. But what happens in practice? How do bankers behave in a crisis when their own money is on the line? Do they behave in a Scrooge-like way, avaricious and tight-fisted, concerned only to recover their own investment, what-ever the social and human cost? Or are they, as they like to see themselves, hard-pressed yet kindly men, anxious to extend a helping hand if possible when trouble looms? If at the end of the day they are forced to pronounce sentence of death, it is only because, they tend to argue, all avenues have already been explored; the patient is already terminally ill and further treatment will not only be very costly but will only serve to postpone the evil day.

As bankers invariably have the final word, for reasons I have already explained, this line of argument is rarely challenged. Once the patient is dead it is very difficult to prove that the bankers' diagnosis was wrong.

But let us look at bankers' power in action. One of the most recent and vivid examples came in the late winter of 1982 when in the space of six weeks the banks pulled the plug on two very large and very different enterprises. The collapse in early February of Sir Freddie Laker's airline business, Laker Airways, described in detail in the next chapter, was a spectacular media event. However much he might have frightened the banks and enraged his competitors – and he did both in good measure – to the general public Sir Freddie was a folk hero: a David battling on behalf of the man in the street against the Goliaths of the international airline business, an image shrewdly exploited by Laker himself.

By contrast Stone-Platt's collapse lacked drama: there were no stranded passengers, no weeping air hostesses marching down Whitehall, and no old ladies were prompted to send their savings to offset a multi-million-pound debt. And yet the fall of Stone-Platt was more significant for a number of reasons. First, it was by far the biggest industrial casualty of the recent recession, an international company with thirty-two separate businesses.

The main impact of the failure was on the textile towns of Lancashire, the company's base for more than a century. But the shock waves were felt across three continents – in Europe where the company had important interests, in the Far East and in North America. The fall of Stone-Platt marked the end of an era: a rite of passage in the long-drawn-out and painful history of Britain's decline as a major manufacturing nation. Second, it was a bitter personal defeat for the chairman, Leslie Pincott, the former and last head of the late lamented Prices and Incomes

Board, who for seventeen months had struggled against the odds to save the company from collapse and who, to this day, firmly believes that victory was only just round the corner. On the day the company collapsed and the receiver was appointed Pincott had to blink back his tears. And when I saw him, nearly two years later, he was still a sad and disappointed man. Third, the banks' decision to put Stone-Platt out of its agony provoked one of the fiercest and most public rows between the institutions and the banks that the City had seen for many years. The rumpus was about bankers' power and the allegation was that it had been used in a manner that was both hasty and irresponsible. Both the M & G unit trust group and Equity Capital for Industry already owned some 20 per cent of Stone-Platt's equity and had promised more when the banks foreclosed. David Hopkinson, the managing director of M & G which was in for £1.5 million, was furious. He told the *Sunday Times* that the banks had been 'bloody-minded' and added: 'When a consortium is trying to rescue a company, you have to find some way of controlling individual members so that they do not act solely in their own interests. . . If anyone had said that the banks were going to withdraw support so soon nobody would have subscribed.' As shareholders both M & G and Equity Capital had lost money so their anger was understandable. But Pincott, a distinguished oil company executive before his stint at the Prices and Incomes Board, had lost more than that: his efforts had been wasted and his prestige as a successful businessman had been damaged. He therefore lashed out at the banks in particular and the receivership process in general. 'In cases where banks have a floating charge and there are no other financial solutions, receivership may still be the only way,' he conceded. 'But in the case of an industrial group with a strong position in various international markets and a fund of engineering skills, it seems to be a crude nineteenth-century solution to a sophisticated twentieth-century problem. In Stone-Platt's case it seems to me more akin to "cannibalism" than surgery. It ignores the rights of employees, of unsecured creditors . . . and of various classes of shareholders. The whole process is governed by the immediacy of realising assets within a very short time scale, and inevitably businesses are sold at less than their real value... In Stone-Platt's case, we had good products, good labour relations, world markets and skills, and a practical plan for survival – and yet the rug was pulled when we were more than halfway through the rescue job. On behalf of a large number of people I submit that this is not good enough.'

Throughout the late 60s and early 70s Stone-Platt was one of the outstanding success stories of British industry with a tradition going back nearly a hundred years. At the height of its glory in the 1920s it employed 30,000 people in Oldham alone; it had its own railway lines and even its own coal mine. Nearly every family in Oldham owed its living one way or another to Stone-Platt, or rather Platt Brothers as it was then called. The merger with the London-based marine engineers, J. Stone, came only in the 1950s. The London headquarters occupied a splendid five-storey building in Mayfair's Grafton Street, of which the top floor was given over entirely to directors' dining rooms and a company flat for the chairman. The head office alone cost £1 million a year to run and the research and development operation, at Helmshore in Lancashire, was also a lavish affair. It was run by the then deputy chairman, Edward Smalley, who came from a long line of Lancashire engineers.

The company, managed by engineers steeped in the textile and engineering traditions of Lancashire, was immensely proud of its prestige and success. And though it was nominally run from the head office in Grafton Street, all important engineering decisions were made by a group nicknamed 'the Lancashire mafia' who ran the three factories at Accrington, Bolton and Oldham and the research and development complex. They were men who had grown up in the business and knew the technical side backwards: they were much less well-versed, however, in the all-important techniques of marketing and finance. Decentralisation was all the rage. So each factory was run as a self-contained unit, only loosely supervised from the centre. And as the operating companies were never charged for the cost of borrowing money, they appeared more profitable than they actually were.

None of these weaknesses, however, was apparent in the early 70s. In 1976 the company reported record pre-tax profits of £15.8 million on a turnover of £113 million. Stone-Platt had become one of the world leaders in the manufacture of textile machinery by selling turnkey plants to the developing world. Where their Swiss and German rivals sold individual pieces of automated, high-value machinery, Stone-Platt offered their customers a total integrated package, from power plant to production line. And as the home market began to decline from the mid-70s onwards Stone-Platt turned increasingly to countries like India, South Korea, Taiwan and Indonesia to keep the production lines in Lancashire running. The company did not depend entirely on Lancashire: to fight off the competition and to offset the decline in the British market it moved into America where in 1973 it bought Saco-Lowell, a well-run textile machinery firm in South Carolina. It also made an important investment in Spain as a means of gaining a foothold in Latin America; and finally it strengthened its British base by purchasing another Lancashire company, J. Scragg, which built highly specialised texturising machinery that put the crinkles in nylon and polyester fibres and had 30 per cent of the world market.

All these moves might have been sensible had it not been for the disastrous collapse of the home market from the mid-70s onwards. For a time this problem was masked by Stone-Platt's export successes in the Far East, but by 1979 it was clear that there were troubles on this front also. Not only had demand switched from Stone-Platt's huge, integrated plants to the more advanced, highly automated one-off machines offered by the Swiss and the Germans, but in the Far East the customers on which Stone-Platt now so heavily relied were, in the wake of the international oil crisis, themselves cutting back. 'Factories were started, buildings went up. But somehow the actual orders for the equipment to fill them kept being postponed,' says Leslie Pincott. 'But instead of cutting back in Lancashire, the "mafia" went on cutting metal. The result was that stocks rose and the warehouses filled up to the point where we eventually had more than £12 million worth of stuff, all packed and stacked with nowhere to go.'

As the crisis deepened, the company, desperate for orders, began to take risks. A Pakistani, living in Liechtenstein, was paid a £650,000 commission to negotiate a £5 million contract in Saudi Arabia. The original site for the plant was seventy miles south of Mecca. On investigation, however, it turned out there was no water there and so the location was switched to another place fifty miles north of Mecca. But though the agent got his commission, the deal never went through and the machinery destined for Saudi Arabia finished up in the Bolton warehouse.

As the problems mounted, so the profits began to crumble. From a high point of £15.8 million in 1976, two years later they were down to £9.5 million, and in 1979 came the first of a series of losses – nearly £3 million. In fact the situation was even worse than the balance sheet revealed for the losses in Lancashire were by now nearly £6 million; a figure partly concealed by the fact that other parts of the group were still trading profitably.

That Lancashire was a problem which could only get worse had been recognised as long ago as 1975. In that year a senior executive, Jimmy McKinnon, a hard-headed production man, had seen the danger and wrote a report recommending that the Lancashire operation should be cut from three factories to one. But opposition from the Lancashire 'mafia' was such that the report never even reached the board. 'Lancashire was a very dug-in sort of place,' Pincott comments sourly. In any event the McKinnon report would probably have fallen on deaf ears as the view of the chairman, Sir Geoffrey Hawkins, and his deputy, Edward Smalley, was that the road to salvation lay not in closing down factories and thus antagonising the trade unions but in diversification. Under Smalley's personal direction the R & D team at Helmshore spent much valuable time and money exploring the possibilities of the carpet business and other ventures far removed from the company's traditional line of business, without noticeable success.

By 1979 as the company plunged into loss the problem of Lancashire could no longer be ignored; and thus the decision was reluctantly taken to close the Oldham factory. Even then the board wavered. The original plan had been to shut Stone's marine engineering factory based at Deptford in London's dockland and transfer the business to Oldham but this was found to be impractical.

These moves took place against the background of a good deal of corporate blood-letting, during which the banks for the first time began to flex their muscles. The deputy managing director, Geoffrey Buckley, who had been brought in some years earlier from Ford to strengthen the financial team, left with a £250,000 golden handshake, to be replaced by Robin Tavener, then head of the successful electrical division. At the same time the banks quietly let it be known that they were unhappy with Edward Smalley who was due to take over as chairman from Sir Geoffrey Hawkins. The fact that Smalley was going through a domestic crisis at the time also appears to have had some bearing on his non-promotion. Nonetheless he continued to play an influential part in the drama that was to come.

The closure of Oldham was a long-drawn-out affair which continued well into 1980, thanks partly to a seven-week strike. Eventually 600 people were laid off at Oldham and another 350 jobs were lost at Accrington and Bolton – so nearly 1000 people, a quarter of the labour force, went that year. But there was to be no relief. A new spinning machine, launched the previous autumn at the Hanover Fair, failed to live up to expectations: not only did it produce thread that was 25 per cent weaker than the competition's but its performance was markedly worse than the machine it was supposed to replace. And it therefore had to be re-engineered.

Just how closely the banks were involved in the decision to close Oldham is not clear. But as the closure of the factory meant that £7,250,000 was wiped off the balance sheet, thus reducing the banks' security by that amount, they were certainly informed. But with thirteen banks involved no one, it seems, was prepared to take the initiative: it was a case of seeking safety in numbers.

The balance sheet was still, at this stage, comparatively healthy and the company was by no means over-borrowed. All the same the cut-backs and reorganisation costs meant that the shareholders' funds, the security against which the banks had lent, had dropped by nearly 15 per cent, or £10 million, in the course of a single year. And when trading losses of £2.9 million were taken into account, the figure was even larger.

The closure of Oldham was meant to save the company. As it turned out, it nearly killed it there and then. Under normal accounting rules the company had to make a provision in the accounts for the Oldham shut-down. But through lack of financial expertise at head office it was done in such a manner that quite by accident it triggered off a default clause in a loan agreement to a small American bank. The financing of Stone-Platt was at this stage a complex affair. Altogether it owed some £30 million to some thirteen separate banks in the UK and overseas, mainly in medium- and long-term loans. But because all these individual loan agreements were tied together by what bankers call 'cross-default' clauses, the accidental breach of the loan agreement to the American bank meant that the entire £30 million became due immediately. Technically Stone-Platt was trading as an insolvent company, an offence which automatically leads to the appointment of the Official Receiver.

This awful discovery, made at 5.55 one Friday afternoon in April 1980, caused a major panic. The problem of resolving the conflicting claims of some thirteen banks was so complex that the deputy governor of the Bank of England, Sir Jasper Hollom, was called in to help sort out the mess. After a hectic series of meetings the week before Easter the crisis was resolved, but only after the banks, now thoroughly alerted to Stone-Platt's financial condition, had extracted much tougher conditions than before. The loans were rescheduled but instead of the money costing 5 per cent, the price was now higher and the repayment period was much shorter. The banks insisted that the loans and overdraft facilities were now on offer only until January 1982, after which the entire package would have to be renegotiated. It was an episode for which the company was later to pay dearly.

Faced with the banks' ultimatum it was now clear, even to the Lancashire 'mafia', that drastic surgery was needed if the group was to overcome the crisis. A report was commissioned from the prestigious Shirley Institute which duly reported that although the company had lost its world leadership in textile machinery design, it was still 'an equal second' in most areas. But as demand was now running at 50 per cent below that of five years before, this was small consolation. In mid-year a company working party was set up to look once again at the Lancashire problem. But as the 'mafia' was heavily represented, nothing was done. As one senior executive said: 'We were frightened of doing anything too drastic because of the unions who had already reacted badly to the decision to close Oldham. You must remember that there were over 2000 people still employed in the two remaining factories and you just can't lay off two-thirds of your workforce overnight.'

But the pressure from the banks was now such that something had to be done. So instead of taking the knife to Lancashire the board looked around for other possibilities. In the end, after much agonising, the axe fell on the profitable pump division which at the end of the year was sold for £11 million to Indian Head, a subsidiary of the German Thyssen group. But the relief was only temporary. When the 1980 accounts were published, they revealed that Lancashire had lost another £7 million and that the cost of reorganising the marine and mechanical engineering divisions which were also being prepared for sale amounted to another £5 million. With the banks' deadline just over a year away, time – and money – were fast running out.

Behind the scenes the Bank of England and the company's merchant bankers, Hill Samuel, were already preparing the ground for a second, more considered, rescue package: one that involved not only the banks but institutional investors like Equity Capital for Industry. By the summer of 1980 it was already clear that the bank facilities lent under the first rescue package that April were not sufficient and that unless someone was prepared to inject fresh equity into the company and thus restore the rapidly rising debt to equity ratio, Stone-Platt would once again be in hock to the bankers.

The problem was not just financial. The City's confidence in the existing management had dwindled almost to vanishing point. And in the autumn of 1980, a well-known firm of headhunters, Tyzack & Partners, was asked to look for a new chairman. He would be part-time, working only two and a half days a week for which he would be paid £15,000 a year, plus fringe benefits such as a chauffeur-driven car and an office for his other interests. The man they found was Leslie Pincott, a former senior executive with Exxon, the American oil company. At this time he was chairman of the Prices and Incomes Board which he was in the process of winding down. The PIB had performed a useful if controversial function in the 60s and 70s. It had been the centrepiece of successive governments' attempts to establish a voluntary incomes policy. But the laissez-faire, monetarist policies of the Thatcher Government meant that it no longer had a useful part to play; and so effectively Leslie Pincott was working himself out of a job.

At the age of fifty-eight Pincott was ready for a new challenge, even one as arduous and as risky as Stone-Platt. An accountant by profession with a clear, cool mind, he had proved himself to be a capable administrator with the PIB, and hoped that if he succeeded in turning Stone-Platt round almost any job in British industry he cared to name would be his for the asking. Most ambitious businessmen would have thought twice about taking on Stone-Platt but Pincott was convinced that given half a chance he could pull it off. His advantages were high intelligence, objectivity and a firm grasp of the financial complexities, but his cool manner masked great emotional involvement and he could, so colleagues say, be a difficult man to work with. 'The trouble with Leslie,' says one man who came to know him well, 'is that as the pressures got worse, he wanted to do everything himself. He had to be restrained from rushing out and selling machinery himself.'

The impact of Pincott's arrival at the Grafton Street headquarters in November 1980 was immediate. It led to yet another corporate reshuffle as Pincott hand-picked his team. It did not include Edward Smalley. Robin Tavener, another accountant who had been with the company since 1969 and who had made a good job of running the electrical division, had already been moved up from deputy managing director to become chief executive. And some weeks after Pincott's arrival Ray Whitfield, a former director of Rolls Royce where he had run the Bristol Siddeley division, was brought in from outside. Officially he was a non-executive deputy chairman but his real job was to sort out Lancashire once and for all.

Pincott's most pressing task was to prepare the ground for the second rescue package on which work had already started before his arrival. Yet another investigation, this time by Price Waterhouse, the City accountants, was commissioned and Sir Henry Benson, the well-known accountant, was enlisted to reduce the number of banks involved to manageable proportions. 'If we were going to arrive at sensible answers, we had to get some of them off the dance floor,' says Pincott. Eventually nine of the thirteen banks were persuaded to bow out leaving only the Midland, Barclays, National Westminster and Williams & Glyn's. The outline of the new deal was fixed by January 1981 but it took another two months of haggling before the final agreement was reached. All in all a further £10 million was to be injected into the company in the form of new equity financed by the institutions: for their part the banks agreed to lend the company up to £40 million; the bulk of it, some £25 million, repayable over the next five years. The basic assumption underlying the whole exercise was that things were now going well in Lancashire and that the textile division, which had lost £13 million over the previous two years, would now break even in 1981. This is what the company told the banks and it was on that understanding that the deal was done. 'This,' said the man from the Midland, 'is a sound commercial decision. We wouldn't make a five-year commitment for up to £25 million as a public relations exercise.'

The Midland might not have been so sanguine, however, if it had known what Ray Whitfield was, even at that moment, discovering in Lancashire. Early in February he had travelled up to Lancashire to be Pincott's eyes and ears. He moved into a small hotel in Accrington and for the next three months delved deep into the affairs of the textile machinery division. Shortly after his arrival Price Waterhouse handed in its report on Lancashire which Pincott had commissioned. And though the accountants found much to criticise they concluded that the picture was not hopeless. They believed that, provided the company immediately implemented a £5 million cost-cutting plan, there was a real possibility that Lancashire might be returned to profit – at best by April 1982 and at worst by January 1983. The accountants recommended that neither Accrington nor Bolton should be closed – at least for the time being. But the ink was hardly dry on the Price Waterhouse report before Whitfield came up with his own very different conclusions. Far from Lancashire breaking even in 1982 as the banks had been told, he reported, it now seemed that the division was heading for a £5 million loss and that there was no alternative but to close at least one of the two remaining factories at Accrington and Bolton. The only question was: which? The dilemma was put to the banks but there was no clear reply. Instead they commissioned their own accountants, Ernst and Whinney, to make the first of three eventual reports into Lancashire which was much less optimistic than the Price Waterhouse exercise. It only served to underline the banks' worries about their security. Throughout the crisis, Pincott says, the banks put forward no ideas of their own. 'The banks did not have a solution,' says Pincott. 'They just wanted their money back.' The financial picture, as presented by the banks' accountants, was bleak but the hard decisions were left to the company to make.

The obvious choice for closure was Accrington, the larger but less efficient of the two plants, but as the shut-down costs were higher, it was Bolton that got the chop instead.

It was a move that led to further conflict in the boardroom. Initially relations between Pincott and Tavener, the chief executive, had been good. But as arguments raged over the Lancashire problem, the two men fell out. They quarrelled, so insiders say, about everything: from where to site the new company headquarters that were to replace the hugely expensive Grafton Street offices, to the size of the company's wine bill. Pincott believed that with the company on its uppers, it was no time for high living. In September of that year, Tavener, who earned £45,000 a year which with pension rights and other fringe benefits was worth £70,000 a year, left the company with a £65,000 golden handshake.

As Pincott struggled to meet the banks' January 1982 deadline for the third and, hopefully, the final rescue operation, the decision was made to sell off what remained of Platt Saco-Lowell, the textile machinery division which was now reduced to the plant at Accrington and the Saco-Lowell factory in North Carolina. In early autumn of 1981 Whitfield was dispatched on a world tour in search of a likely buyer.

Pincott favoured either the Germans or Lord Weinstock's General Electric but in fact there was only one real candidate: John Hollingsworth of J. D. Hollingsworth and Wheels of Greenville, South Carolina. A Southern, Bible-punching Baptist who never wore a tie and began all business meetings with prayers, John Hollingsworth was one of the real originals of the textile business. He had inherited the company from his father who began by selling material to Saco-Lowell, Stone-Platt's US subsidiary, from a handcart at the gates of the factory. But over the years he had built up a hugely successful business. It was Pincott himself who opened the negotiations with Hollingsworth but the two men were so very different that they never really established a rapport. Whitfield and Hollingsworth did. And after long prayerful meetings at an hotel in Atlanta, punctuated by even longer pauses while the Hollingsworth team withdrew for private consultations, a deal was finally struck in March 1982. It was agreed that the two textile machinery plants in America and Lancashire, which was all that now remained of Platt Saco-Lowell, the once proud textile machinery division, should be sold for £12.75 million.

With the Hollingsworth agreement on the point of signature Pincott firmly believed that at long last the end of the tunnel was in sight. The company was a mere shadow of its former self. In a little over eighteen months the entire textile machinery division had either been closed or sold off with the loss of 3500 jobs; and profitable activities such as the marine and pumps divisions had also been sold off. But in financial terms the price had been crippling. The closures and the losses meant that something like £70 million had been wiped off the balance sheet in a little over three years with a corresponding reduction in the banks' security. Even so Pincott was convinced that now that the cancer that was Lancashire had been cut out, the company could survive. The money from Hollingsworth and another £5 million from a sale and lease-back operation on the electrical division's factory at Crawley would, he calculated, have cut the borrowings almost exactly in half. The institutional shareholders apparently thought so too for they agreed, as their part in the final rescue package, to inject between £5 million and £7 million in fresh equity. The snag was, however, that this money would not be available for another six months – until the autumn of 1982. Meanwhile it was the banks who were still owed £34 million who would have to take the strain. It was at this point, in early March 1982, that the worm turned.

On March 11, Pincott was summoned to an interview with the general manager of the Midland, the lead bank, and told that unless the company could immediately find another £15 million in new equity from somewhere, the bank would appoint a receiver. It was to prove an impossible request. Seven days later, the receiver, Bill Mackey of Ernst and Whinney, moved in with 120 staff and began to dismember the company. The Hollingsworth deal and Crawley sale and lease back, two vital ingredients in Pincott's own rescue plan, were temporarily shelved as Mackey himself took over responsibility. But as Hollingsworth himself was already in London, about to sign a deal with Stone-Platt, negotiations were quickly resumed but this time with Mackey in charge. After a marathon session which lasted until four o'clock in the morning, Platt Saco-Lowell was sold to Hollingsworth on exactly the same terms as had been negotiated with Stone-Platt. But other assets were sold off at prices which were way below what they would have fetched had the company still been in business. It was a vivid example of the banks' 'gone concern' approach.

The Midland may have been the messenger but it was, by all accounts, Stan Carslake of Barclays, who had been sceptical throughout, who actually delivered the final blow. 'He didn't exactly say no in so many words,' says Pincott. 'But he made it very clear that he thought the company should be broken up and relaunched under new, more vigorous management. I did not entirely disagree. In a sense that is exactly what I was trying to do. What I objected to was the manner in which it was done. My plan, which would have saved the company, was not given a chance. It was never seriously looked at by the senior people in the banks who relied on the judgement of junior accountants who were too young to know anything about the risk business. They could see lots of black and very little white. The banks were not really interested in the company's future. At the end of the day all they were interested in was their security. And the irony is that by the time they had pulled the plug they were no longer really at risk at all. Their loans were well covered. The only people who have lost out have been the unsecured creditors, the shareholders and, of course, most of the employees.' In defence of his thesis Pincott points to the subsequent history of the electrical division at Crawley where events closely followed the plan he had already laid down. Some months later the carcass of the electrical company, stripped bare by the receiver of all debts and all cash, was sold to none other than Pincott's old adversary, Robin Tavener, the former chief executive, for £15 million. The money was raised in the City by a concern called Candover which specialised in company reconstructions. To finance his parcel of 100,000 shares Tavener used his golden handshake, sold his London flat and took out a second mortgage on his home at Brighton. At one point Tavener was paying out £1000 a month. But the risk has paid off. The company, now renamed Stone International, which specialises in providing equipment for mass transit systems throughout the world, is now more profitable than ever before and in the autumn of 1984 it was floated on the London Stock Exchange. After more than twenty years in the business Tavener looks like becoming a very rich man: the one bright spot in a sad story.

But did it have to turn out like this? Is Pincott right when he accuses the banks of lack of imagination and of an obsession with their own security? The record shows that the banks were not unhelpful. Twice, within the space of two years, they had come to the rescue. But on the third time of asking, they lost their nerve. They had seen the company miss its forecasts too often to be willing to give it another chance and were not prepared to back Pincott's assertion that success was just around the corner. 'Why should we have been asked to take all the risk and let the institutional investors who were putting up the equity take all the profit?' Barclays' Stan Carslake protests. It is a classic statement of the banks' position. And yet at the end of the day, it was not the banks who lost. Bill Mackey and his team eventually recovered more than enough from the wreckage for the banks to be repaid in full and so the depositors' money was safe. Nor had the company, unlike the third world countries to which the banks have lent so freely, ever defaulted on its interest payments. What was lost through a mixture of managerial incompetence, worldwide recession and bankers' caution was what had once been one of the proudest names in British engineering. Such a loss is impossible to quantify.

9 The Man who Fell to Earth

IN FEBRUARY 1981, almost exactly a year before he went bust, Sir Freddie Laker took a step which he hoped would lead to his airline, already the world's largest independent, becoming a major force on the international scene. Encouraged by an interest rate subsidy from the British Government which, for political reasons, was keen to see the sale go through, he bought three A300 European Airbuses, the new Anglo-French wide-bodied jets, that were to be the spearhead of his attack on the rich, over-protected European market. Nearly all of the $131 million required was provided by a consortium, led by the Midland, of thirteen British and European banks. Later the Midland was to say that it had not been keen on the idea and had only agreed to participate after some arm-twisting by the Government. As summer came, the Midland explained to its fellow consortium members that it had always known that Laker's creditworthiness was poor and that the balance sheet did not look good but that the money had been loaned on the basis of the value of the aircraft. Whatever the bankers' misgivings, however, they were not expressed. In fact the loan was over-subscribed – a tribute to Freddie Laker's magnetism and power of persuasion. With the benefit of hindsight, City people now question the role of the banks in the Laker collapse. 'Laker may have made mistakes but the banks have a good deal to answer for,' says Ian McIntosh of Samuel Montagu, the merchant bankers, who played a key role in Laker's final days. 'They must have been aware of the risks but even so they were more than prepared to put up the money. It's really quite extraordinary.'

The Laker story, however, is much more than the simple and

by now familiar tale of bankers wading in too deeply and then being forced to swim for their lives. The cast is larger and the story more colourful and more complicated. The conventional view is that Laker was to a very large extent the author of his own misfortunes. A character larger than life, with an astonishing ability to get his message across and so capture the imagination of ordinary people, he is widely thought, like Icarus, to have flown too high and to have paid the penalty for his daring or, as some would say, recklessness. In this there is a good deal of truth. But there is another aspect to the saga which has yet to be fully explored. However popular Sir Freddie may have been with his customers, within the airline business itself he made many powerful enemies: manufacturers, airline executives, tour operators and travel agents all had their reasons for disliking him intensely. And so when the crisis broke in the summer of 1981 there were many who saw in Laker's difficulties a heaven-sent opportunity to rid themselves of a very troublesome competitor. The fact that Laker himself had provided them with the weapons to do the deed is beside the point. What needs to be examined very carefully is the precise role played by all the actors in the drama, especially the major airlines who had suffered most at Laker's hands.

Since launching his hugely popular Skytrain service under the slogan 'Fly me, I'm Freddie' in 1977, after a bitter, six-year legal battle with the British Government and the major carriers, Laker had established himself as a force to be reckoned with on the North Atlantic. Skytrain was a novel, simple concept. Though later modified, initially it was run on a first-come, first-served basis. There were no reservations and no frills; customers either brought their own food or paid for it on the plane. The service was both convenient and, above all, cheap. The cost of a round trip to New York by Skytrain was £123, compared to £392 with any of the scheduled services. By under-cutting its competitors by nearly 70 per cent Laker Airways had become the sixth largest carrier on the North Atlantic, bigger than the Swiss, the French, the Canadians and the Scandinavians; he was already running neck and neck with the Dutch and only America's TWA and Pan Am, the Germans' Lufthansa and the state-subsidised British Airways were ahead.

It was by any standards a remarkable achievement for a man who had started his commercial life a quarter of a century before as a market gardener in the fruit orchards of Kent. Having smashed, as he thought, the price-fixing cartel on the North Atlantic and having brought international air travel within the reach of the ordinary working man, Sir Freddie, knighted by the Callaghan Government two and a half years before, now set his sights on Europe, the richest and most protected cartel of all. Not only were prices higher in Europe than anywhere else in the world but the profit margins were enormous. A 50 per cent mark-up over operating costs was standard practice. Since then there has been a proliferation of special, under-the-counter deals as airlines have unloaded their spare seats on the bucket shops. But in 1981 the cartel was still more or less intact. 'I want to get a can opener on Europe,' Laker said. 'It has taken me more than thirty years to get to America. I'll be dead before I get a Skytrain into Europe.' The price war on the North Atlantic had served to highlight just how unrealistic European prices had become. A 1000-mile round trip from London to Frankfurt, for example, cost twice as much on a regular scheduled flight as the 6000-mile excursion to New York and back. And so, flushed with the apparent success of Skytrain, Laker announced his intention to do battle with the big carriers on virtually every major European route. From his base at Gatwick he intended to serve, he said, no fewer than thirty-six European cities, from Stockholm to Las Palmas, linked together by a network of 630 separate routes.

For what was essentially a one-man-band backed by a small but technically highly competent team of engineers and mechanics, it was a bold gesture. And to bring it off Laker needed to expand his already tightly stretched, shoestring operation in every direction. He would need more money, more staff, more planes, and, most important of all, indulgence and support from a disparate but ever-growing army of bankers in the UK, the US, Japan and Europe.

When Skytrain took to the air in September 1977 the Laker

fleet consisted of two ancient Boeing 707s, four BAC 1-11s, and four McDonnell Douglas DC10s, three of which Laker had bought at a knock-down price from Mitsui, the Japanese trading company. Here Laker had had a stroke of luck. The Mitsui DC10s had originally been intended for the Japanese domestic airline, All-Nippon. But thanks to the intervention of the Japanese Prime Minister, Takeo Fukuda, on whom the rival Lockheed had put improper pressure – a scandal which led to his resignation – All-Nippon ordered the Lockheed Tri-Star instead and Mitsui was left with the DC10s on its hands. It was therefore more than happy to sell the planes to Laker on very favourable terms. The $59 million for the first two planes was to be repaid at 6 per cent over ten years and the rate for the third plane was even more generous. What is more the loan was backed 100 per cent by the Japanese Government. The remaining DC10 was bought direct from McDonnell Douglas and financed rather more conventionally by the Clydesdale Bank, a subsidiary of the Midland in London.

But Laker was not content to stop there. In 1978 he raised the ante once again by ordering five brand-new DC10s from the makers, McDonnell Douglas, which were delivered between December 1979 and the following June. It was a huge order. The £228 million dollar deal was financed by a consortium led by US EXIM bank in Washington and underwritten by the US Government and the two manufacturers, McDonnell Douglas and the US engine makers General Electric, who were later to play a vital part in the story. This time there were no special terms. For the first time in his career Laker was having to pay full market rate. And even more ominously the deal was denominated in dollars while Laker's earnings were very largely in pounds. In the past this had worked to Laker's advantage. In 1982 *The Sunday Times* calculated on the basis of then unpublished accounts that out of profits of £2.2 million in the previous financial year no less than £1.5 million came from foreign exchange transactions. But with the pound falling the pendulum was beginning to swing the other way, with consequences that were to prove quite disastrous.

If Laker and the bankers were aware of this risk they gave no sign. Laker was so set on achieving his European ambition that he not only concluded the deal with EXIM and the other DC10 lenders but he plunged ahead with the Airbuses as well. The financial impact on Laker Airways of these two deals was enormous and to any prudent banker should have been frightening. At this time Laker Airways was still only a medium-sized, privately owned company in which the joint owners, Laker and his first wife Joan, had subscribed no more than £510,000. And yet the company had borrowed over £250 million, on which the capital and interest payments amounted to some £45 million a year out of a total cash flow of £130 million. By any standards the company was dangerously over-borrowed, had too much capacity, was too dependent on the North American market and very vulnerable if for any reason the Atlantic route turned sour. Questions were asked about where the company was going to find the money but Laker always brushed these aside with typical panache. 'It's not my money,' he was accustomed to reply. But what happens if anything goes wrong? 'In that case,' Laker would reply, 'you will simply get your fucking aircraft back.' There had already been some nasty moments. In May 1979 an American Airlines DC10 crashed shortly after take-off from Chicago's O'Hare airport killing all 274 people aboard. It was the worst disaster in American airline history and the American authorities responded by grounding the entire DC10 fleet, including Laker's aircraft. It eventually transpired that the fault was not in the plane itself but in American Airlines' maintenance procedures: to save time and money the engines had been crudely refitted by using a fork-lift truck instead of a special jig provided by the makers, thus cracking the mountings which attached the engine to the wing. Under the stress of take-off the port engine broke loose, severing the flight controls. As a result the pilot was helpless: the plane rolled over and plunged into the ground.

The accident could not have happened at a worse moment, right at the beginning of the peak holiday season. Laker's faith in the much-criticised plane did not waver – something for which the makers, McDonnell Douglas, who saw the sales of the DC10s plummet after the crash, were profoundly grateful. But the six-week episode cost Laker, so he later calculated, between £10 and £15 million in lost revenues. Again there were worries about Laker's financial health and again they were dismissed. 'No, I'm not bust,' Laker declared. 'The strength of our balance sheet will see us through.' A year later came a second blow to the all-important Atlantic market when American air traffic controllers went on strike.

These setbacks, however, were minor in comparison with what was to come. The world economy was feeling the effect of the 1979 oil price rises with the result that the boom in transatlantic air travel was slackening off. Faced with massive over-capacity all the major airlines plunged into the red. By 1981 IATA, the industry's ruling body, reckoned that its members were losing a billion dollars; the North Atlantic alone accounted for £600 million. All the majors were feeling the strain: Pan Am was in such deep financial trouble that its own survival was in question and British Airways only kept going with the help of large Government loans. One of the ironies of the Laker story is that the very day his company went bust, the British Government announced further assistance for the state-owned airline. Competition, already fierce, became cut-throat as everybody cut fares in a desperate attempt to win a greater share of a sagging market.

THE CRISIS — THE FIRST STAGE

In June 1981, just five months after the triumphant conclusion of the Airbus deal, the first cracks in the edifice that Laker had built began to appear. Financial control was not one of the strong points of the Laker operation but the one set of figures that was watched closely was the monthly traffic returns; up to May Laker had just about been holding his own on the North Atlantic. The figures for the first five months were slightly down on the previous year but then so were everybody else's. But it was the June figures that were the real shocker: suddenly Laker's share of the market had collapsed. While everybody else was more or less holding their own his traffic was down to 40 per cent of the previous year and, what was worse, projections of forward sales in North America were even bleaker. This development took Laker totally by surprise and his first reaction was to blame the staff and goad them to further effort. They were told that no new equipment would be bought or fresh staff hired. 'There must be something wrong with the product,' Laker said. But when July and August brought further bad news Laker had no option but to pay an urgent call on his bankers. The next instalments of the money he had borrowed for the DC10s and the Airbuses were due in mid-September and though Laker said he could just about meet the $12 million bill, he could foresee a total cash flow problem for the current financial year ending March 1982 of between £18 and £23 million. Laker was not actually out of cash: he still had, he said, between £14 million and £17 million in the bank, largely on overdraft. But the decline in the pound from $2.30 to $1.80 had cost him £9 million. And he was afraid that if the banks were unwilling to help then what he described as 'a controlled sale' of the airline was a real possibility. In an effort to raise cash he had already decided to put the old Boeing 707s and the BAC 1-11s, the backbone of his original fleet, on to the market. 'This is the first time in thirty-four years,' he told the banks, 'that I have ever taken a cash flow problem to my bankers.'

So far Laker's troubles were known only to those most intimately involved. But word was beginning to spread. Early in August the *Wall Street Journal* published a piece headlined 'Laker seeking to reschedule dollar debts'; debts it put at $455.2 million. Somebody had talked. It was at a meeting at the Savoy Hotel on August 18 that matters first came to a head. Altogether there were fifty-three people present: Laker and his wife, all the Laker directors and representatives of all the major creditors, with the exception of the EXIM bank and the US Private Export Funding Corporation (PEFCO). Laker was in a surprisingly buoyant mood. He told the assembled throng that there were, as far as he could see, three ways out of the crisis: 1. To defer the next two capital payments on the DC10 and Airbus loans, due in September 1981 and March 1982, totalling £55.3 million, for another twelve months. 2. To amend the loan agreements to allow Laker to repay when the pound had hopefully recovered and times were better. 3. That the banks should club together and give him a fresh £25 million line of credit. Of the three alternatives, Laker preferred the last.

The banks were not so sure. The next day, August 19, the Airbus consortium held a council of war at the Midland. All thirteen banks were represented: among them, the French, Banque Française du Commerce Extérieur, Banque Nationale de Paris, Société Générale, the Germans, Bayerische Verein and the Dresdner, the Austrians, Credit Anstalt, the Canadians, the Royal Bank of Canada, the Americans, the Citibank, and of course the Midland and its subsidiary and long-time Laker backer, the Clydesdale. The bankers had not been impressed by the Laker performance the previous day. There was, they felt, much more involved than a simple exchange rate problem. And all agreed that Laker would, as they put it, 'be in a hole' for 1981/2. They had already asked Laker for more detailed financial information. They wanted a cash flow projection assuming no capital repayments on the loans in 1982; another on the assumption that the repayments were made; and an assessment of the impact on the business of the three Airbuses which had already been delivered.

But the immediate question as the lead banker in the consortium, the Midland, summed up, was: what to do. Dennis Kitching, the general manager, suggested that they were no worse off than when they decided to lend the Airbus money in the first place. If Laker's traffic picked up and he was awarded the European routes he was looking for, there was every reason to believe that Laker Airways would be a good, viable airline. But there was no way, the Midland said, that it was going to give Laker the fresh line of credit he had asked for as his assets were already encumbered by the existing loans. So rescheduling, the bank argued, was the only answer. But for how long and on what terms? These questions remained unanswered. And ominously for Laker the Germans and the Austrians remained conspicuously silent.

From the start it was clear that one of the main problems in the rescue attempt was going to be how to keep the two groups of bankers, the DC10 syndicate in Washington and the Airbus consortium in London, marching in step. Also involved were the Japanese even though they played a rather passive role. As we shall see, each group (and each in itself was far from homogeneous) had its own separate and sometimes very different objectives and as the crisis deepened the groups pulled in different and conflicting directions.

The first indications of the split came only two days after the war council at the Midland. On August 21 the DC10 creditors met in Washington under the chairmanship of William H. Draper, the president of the EXIM bank, whose exposure at that time was just under $150 million. The airframe and engine manufacturers, McDonnell Douglas and General Electric, were in for just under $60 million between them. Their involvement was not only financial: if Laker survived they could count on him for further much needed orders and they therefore had every incentive to be generous. The same argument should in theory have applied to the Airbus manufacturers, British Aerospace and France's Airbus Industrie but as they were looking to the European airlines as their main customers for the new plane, they were much more vulnerable to pressure from Laker's competitors – as events were later to prove.

The DC10 meeting in Washington did not go well for Laker. Bill Draper, EXIM's president, took a particularly tough line. The most he would initially agree to was that the payment due in September should be rolled forward by no more than thirty days. Later Draper was to describe the entire rescheduling exercise as 'a gamble' and said that if Laker wanted to survive the only thing he could do was to cut operational costs, bring in fresh equity and sell the Airbuses. In the event, however, he proved to be more flexible and more understanding than the faction-ridden European bankers.

As the talks dragged on through September with no clear-cut resolution to the rescheduling problem, thanks largely to the stone-walling by the Germans and the Austrians, the Midland was becoming more and more uneasy. On September 21 the bank gave Laker an ultimatum: he was told that he had until the end of December to dispose of the Airbuses plus two or three of the DC10s. And though the consequences if Laker did not comply were never clearly spelled out, privately the Midland was warning that if its partners would not agree the rescheduling programme by then the bank would have to pull the plug.

To this Laker replied that, however logical this solution might seem to the bankers, they did not understand the airline business. The state of the market was such, he argued, that it was just not possible in the present environment to sell off aircraft without incurring substantial losses. He realised that the banks could not and would not do more to help. So he suggested instead that the three manufacturers, McDonnell Douglas, General Electric and Airbus Industrie, should be asked to chip in with a $20 million loan. But as he was in no position to provide the collateral for the money this proposal too fell on deaf ears.

On November 4 the Airbus consortium met again at the Midland's headquarters in the City, where the screw was tightened still further. There was only one outside observer at the meeting, Ray Colgate, a senior official of the Civil Aviation Authority, but his presence was both significant and ominous. The CAA is the body set up by the Government to regulate and license the British airline business. No operator can fly without CAA approval. As a matter of routine the CAA regularly monitors the finances of all British airlines and under the 1982 Civil Aviation Act it has powers to withdraw a licence if it ceases to be satisfied with an airline's financial state of health.

The CAA had been keeping a careful eye on Laker. 'It was,' says Colgate, 'an airline about which we had had some measure of concern for at least a couple of years before the crash. Laker was expanding rapidly but was very heavily borrowed in dollars while most of its income was in pounds.' Colgate first mentioned these anxieties to Laker in mid-summer. 'By June,' Colgate says, 'we could see from his figures that there were going to be some quite substantial shortfalls. We were not so worried about the present situation – until the last day he was still trading legally though it was at times a close-run thing. No, we were more worried about the future.' The CAA confided these fears to David Walker, the industrial director at the Bank of England, who, from about August onwards, began to play an influential part in the drama by acting as a referee and putting strong but discreet pressure on the quarrelling bankers to reconcile their differences.

On August 27 the CAA called Laker in and told him that if the bankers could not agree to reschedule then the CAA might have to revoke his licence. Initially the CAA advised the bankers on the meaning of Laker's traffic figures, which the money men found hard to interpret. But as the crisis intensified Colgate was to play an increasingly important role.

The November 4 meeting at the Midland was a gloomy affair. Ian McIntosh of the merchant bankers, Samuel Montagu, brought in by the Midland to give Laker some badly needed financial advice, reported that Laker's financial condition was now quite desperate: there was not enough cash coming in to enable Laker to meet the repayment schedule on the loans, and the company was facing a £12 million loss for the financial year ending March 1982. Time was running out, McIntosh said. The next tranche of loan money, already twice postponed, was due for repayment on November 15, less than a fortnight away, and unless everybody agreed that Laker should be allowed to defer the capital repayments on the loans for a year, McIntosh argued, the airline would have to stop trading within the very near future. Even then, McIntosh warned, the company could only be saved if the Airbuses were sold, a new financial management team brought in and fresh capital injected. As a stopgap the banks put in Bill Morrison of Thomson McLintock, the accountancy firm, to act as Laker's personal financial adviser for a fee of £750 a day. For its part Samuel Montagu was later to present a bill of £50,000. Even when faced with this stark picture, the banks could not agree. From Washington came the message that EXIM Bank was still holding out for no more than a six-month deferral, while the Germans and the Austrians strongly held to the view that Laker was already past saving and that all this talk of rescheduling was a waste of time. In this the Germans and the Austrians were perhaps being less than dispassionate. In the first place they had lent heavily to Poland and were badly hit by the Polish debt crisis which was fast reaching a climax, culminating in the declaration of martial law only five weeks later on December 13, 1981. For the Germans and the Austrians, one rescheduling was quite enough. Furthermore there were strong institutional links between the German and Austrian banks and the German airline Lufthansa, which was violently opposed to Laker's European plans. Among the other members of the Airbus consortium the suspicion grew that, behind the scenes, Lufthansa was playing an unhelpful role. Only one ray of hope emerged from this meeting: an analysis of Laker's figures showed that if he did manage to pull through until the following spring, the forecast was that if all went well there might be a £13 million profit for 1982/3.

This forecast was outdated even before it had been made. On October 8 Pan Am had declared war on Laker by announcing that, as from November 1, it was going to cut its regular transatlantic fare by 64 per cent to match Laker's prices dollar for dollar. At one stroke the complicated fare structure with its plethora of discounts and special deals was dramatically simplified. From now on there would be just three classes of fare: first, business and economy, set at $261 which was precisely what Laker was charging. Pan Am's lead was immediately followed by TWA and British Airways. It was a tactic that was later to trigger a $1 billion civil suit by the Laker liquidator for damages and a criminal investigation by the anti-trust division of the US Justice Department. In the US, so-called 'predatory pricing' is an offence under the anti-trust Sherman Act. The only defence is that under the Bermuda Two agreement of 1980 which regulates international airline competition, carriers are allowed to match the fares charged by the most efficient in the industry. But even this loophole is hedged about with restrictions, for the agreement goes on to say that fares must also be consistent 'with a high standard of safety and an adequate return to efficient airlines'. There was plenty of scope for argument here. If slimline Laker was unable to make a profit what hope was there for a huge, over-burdened operation like Pan Am which itself was being forced to sell assets to stay aloft?

To Laker and to British Caledonian, who both protested vigorously to the CAA, Bermuda Two was merely a fig leaf to cover a piece of naked aggression by Pan Am. In a letter to the Department of Trade, British Caledonian argued that Pan Am's action was 'predatory' and 'economically suicidal'. The Thatcher Government, however, was unsympathetic, believing as it did in competition whatever the cost. 'Don't forget,' said Ian Sproat, the Aviation Minister, 'that it was a British airline, Laker Airways, that started off this very low fare to the great benefit of the consumer. And if Pan Am can come along and match that and be economic, as it says, well, it's all for the benefit of the consumer.' Pan Am may have convinced the British Government that the new fares were economic but there is not a shadow of doubt that the real reason for the move was to put the knife into Laker. As Pan Am's chief executive, William Waltrip, told a trade paper while on a visit to London a few days later: 'We have to put the fares down to make sure the competition understands that there are not going to be any niches for them anymore. That means to make them understand what the competitive market place is going to be and if they understand that, I think the rates will go up.' Laker was not mentioned by name but it was obvious that it was Laker he had in mind.

The Pan Am move was a blow which struck at the very heart of the Laker operation. He had only survived through his ability to undercut the big boys. Now that price advantage was gone, and he had very little else to offer. And once rumours of his troubles began to spread his troubles mounted. The travel agents and tour operators, energetically wooed by Laker's rivals in the charter and package holiday business, delayed their bookings, concerned lest Laker would be unable to fulfil his obligations. Many had been badly caught in the Court Line crash seven years before and were not anxious to repeat the experience. Confidence in Laker, already low, was falling day by day.

It took some weeks for the effects of Pan Am's pre-emptive strike to become apparent. But when the November figures came in they were terrible: Laker's business on the North Atlantic had been cut by half compared with the year before. Yet the bankers struggled on with, amazingly, something that was beginning to look like success. With the rescheduling talks stalemated, McDonnell Douglas and General Electric decided that the time had come to take the initiative. What alarmed them was the prospect of Laker losing his licence, which in turn would mean the loss of the £60 million they themselves had invested. And so, very cautiously, the two American firms put forward their own rescue plan. The Americans initially offered a new £9.75 million line of credit but only on condition that the Midland increased its overdraft to £7 million, which the Americans said they would guarantee. What worried the Americans most of all was the failure, as they saw it, of the Airbus consortium to do its bit. They saw themselves trapped in a European power play from which there appeared to be no escape. 'I cannot emphasise too strongly,' wrote James McMillan, president of McDonnell Douglas Finance Corporation, 'the concern that we at McDonnell Douglas have at the failure thus far of the Airbus syndicate to go along with the other lenders. The failure is continuing to delay the conclusion of the existing negotiations and we earnestly hope that the Airbus syndicate led by the Midland will quickly reach a satisfactory resolution of the matter by agreeing to a deferral already accepted by other lenders.' (This was a reference to the fact that the DC10 lenders had by now agreed to roll forward their part of the loan for a full twelve months.) 'The failure,' McMillan continued, 'of a relatively small number of banks to agree to the position reached by the majority is prejudicing the interests of all concerned.'

That letter was written on Tuesday, December 15, which proved to be a day of frantic activity for all concerned. The latest Laker figures had just arrived and a posse of civil servants from the Bank of England, the CAA, the Treasury and the Department of Trade and Industry met to consider them. The immediate conclusion was that they were so bad that all the numbers would have to be revised, and unless the bankers could come up with something by Friday, December 18, the Bank of England and the CAA decided Laker would have to be shut down.

This pressure galvanised the Americans. On the Thursday, the day before the deadline, McDonnell Douglas and General Electric came up with a new plan. There were three main features:

1. That the Americans should shoulder some of the risk themselves by taking a £5 million equity stake in Laker Airways
   and convert their debt into preference shares.
2. That British Aerospace and Airbus Industrie should buy back
   the three Airbuses with no loss to Laker thus relieving him of
   an immediate £13 million debt burden.
3. That the Midland's subsidiary Clydesdale should increase its
   overdraft facility from £7 million to £9 million until September 14, 1982.

The overdraft and the cash provided by the Americans, £13.8
million in all, would not solve Laker's long-term problems but it
would give him some desperately needed breathing space. It
took some days to agree the final details of the package. But by
Christmas Eve Ian McIntosh of Samuel Montagu, the bank
which had been co-ordinating the exercise, was convinced that
Laker had been saved. 'We all breathed a huge sigh of relief and
went off to enjoy our Christmas dinners,' he recalls. Laker too
was understandably overjoyed. In a characteristic overstatement
he said: 'It is the best Christmas present of all time. We have
secured our long-term future. We aren't going to lurch from one
crisis to another.' But what nobody, including Laker, had
reckoned on was just how violent the reaction of the airlines
would be.

DID HE FALL OR WAS HE PUSHED?

The exact details of the rescue package were not officially
announced. The involvement of McDonnell Douglas and General Electric was meant to be a secret. In the week before
Christmas, even before the outlines had been agreed, whispers
reached British Caledonian and Dan Air that something was
afoot. But it was not until after the Christmas break that it
began to dawn on the Americans that they might have stuck
their necks out further than was prudent. The proposed £5
million stake in Laker was not in itself large. But the capital base
was so small that even this sum would effectively give the

Americans both a seat on the board and a controlling interest in the British airline. Laker was of course far from being the only customer for the DC10. And though they needed his business badly the consequences of offending virtually every major airline had to be weighed most carefully.

It was just before the New Year that the alarm bells began to ring. The first to get cold feet was General Electric. On December 29 Joe Gallina, a London-based lawyer from the General Electric Finance Corporation, telexed Ian McIntosh at Samuel Montagu to say that under no circumstances was the company's name to be used in any press release. The reference to McDonnell Douglas/General Electric support should be changed, he suggested, to 'DC10 suppliers'. The image problem also worried the publicity men at McDonnell Douglas. 'We can't exactly deny these stories,' one of the PR men, Geoffrey Norris, noted. 'But is it possible to present the story in such a way as to make it appear we are not doing anything out of the ordinary?' On January 5 came a call to McDonnell Douglas from Alistair Pugh, the managing director of British Caledonian, to complain about the American company's sympathetic attitude to Laker and saying that he would take the matter up with the president of Douglas Aircraft, John Brizendine.

It was about this time that a senior McDonnell Douglas official in London, W. E. Kraemer, alerted the top management in California to the dangers of the course on which they were embarked. In a memo headed 'Points for Consideration' he warned that 'the environment in which Laker will have to operate now is significantly less favourable than when the deal was first mooted.' When Laker accepted the Airbuses, Kraemer said, the other airlines began slashing their charter rates, resulting in an environment where Air Europe and Dan Air 'were actively pursuing a course to make life as difficult as possible for Laker'. Dan Air, Kraemer said, was attempting to lease and purchase every BAC 1-11 to add capacity to its own fleet because concern over Laker was forcing tour operators to look to Dan Air for the summer season. Dan Air, Kraemer reported, had received numerous inquiries from tour operators who were hesitating to book until Dan Air's capacity had been checked out. (In other words they were willing to switch from Laker but only after they were sure that Dan Air was able to take their business.) The overall strategy of the charter airlines, Kraemer said, seemed to be to weaken the trade's confidence in the Laker package. The object of his memo, Kraemer concluded, was not to undermine the McDonnell Douglas rescue operation but 'to draw attention to the fact that there was no quick and easy fix to the Laker situation and that Laker's future would be determined in the marketplace rather than in the boardrooms of financial institutions.'

The immediate effect of the airline pressure was to slow the tempo of the rescue negotiations. Although there were still a number of technical problems, in essence the whole deal hinged on McDonnell Douglas and General Electric honouring their pledge to inject their promised £5 million, £4 million from McDonnell Douglas and £1 million from GE. The bankers made it quite clear that if the money did not come, everything would fall apart: the Airbus manufacturers would renege on their promise to buy back the Airbuses and the Midland would not increase the overdraft. On January 11 the Bank of England put its foot down, saying that it wanted an oral but absolute commitment from McDonnell Douglas that it would indeed produce the cash. Meanwhile the Airbus creditors were quarrelling amongst themselves about who would get what and when, when the planes were sold, and all the time Laker's trading position was going from bad to worse. The CAA, which was by now monitoring the figures almost daily, concluded that in addition to the money already agreed, Laker would now need another £5 million 'headroom' if he was to get through what Ray Colgate called 'the March narrows', when pressures on Laker's cash flow would be greatest.

The first to break ranks was General Electric. On January 20 the press caught up with the story. Articles appeared in the *Wall Street Journal*, the *Financial Times* and the *Frankfurter Rundschau*. The *FT* piece was headlined 'US groups take stake in Laker' and mentioned both McDonnell Douglas and General Electric.

The airlines responded to this unwelcome news with a

blizzard of telephone calls, telegrams and telexes, later to be known as 'nastygrams', which left no doubt as to their feelings. One of the first came from Yvan Goosens of Sabena, the Belgian airline, who called Geoffrey Norris, the McDonnell Douglas PR man in London, to express his company's 'amazement and disappointment that McDonnell Douglas should try and prevent the natural demise of a man who had caused other airlines so many problems'. The reaction of René Lapautre, the chairman of UTA, the French airline, was equally strong. In a telex addressed to Brian Rowe, the head of GE's engine division in Cincinnati, Ohio, he said:

> I am addressing you as a long-standing client of your company with which UTA has done business valued at millions of dollars. I am extremely upset by the information about the intended commitment of your company in Laker Airways. This is a fundamental departure from the established neutral position of a manufacturer which cannot be accepted. Furthermore it is ironical that you would provide direct support to the one who openly and knowingly generated the disastrous crisis we are in. It would be outrageous to the whole air transport industry, and particularly to your clients who are providing funds to your company. Such a decision on your part would undoubtedly bear consequences on our future relationship and I do hope you will avoid entering such an undesirable situation – best regards, R. Lapautre, chairman.

The chairman of UTA was not content with an isolated outburst. Simultaneously he sent telexes to the chief executives of Lufthansa, Swissair, KLM, Sabena, SAS, Alitalia and British Caledonian. The Americans' move was, he said, 'totally unacceptable' and suggested that 'we make known to the presidents of McDonnell Douglas and General Electric our opposition.'

The airlines duly responded as requested. On February 2 there descended on the heads of McDonnell Douglas and General Electric an immense wave of protest from virtually every major European carrier. As W. E. Kraemer of McDonnell Douglas noted in a long telex sent to his masters in St Louis that same day:

> It is now clear that the vehemence of the opposition to Laker and directed against MDC for our perceived role in creating a potential solution to the Laker financial problem has spread from the direct charter air carriers in the UK such as Dan Air, Britannia, Air UK etc., beyond the earlier identified opposition from B.Cal, *on an orchestrated basis* [my italics] throughout Europe to most of the scheduled carriers. As was indicated in previous discussions the Laker filing of 666 point-to-point fares intra Europe which he proposed to serve with the A-300 Airbus fleet and the ultra-low I.T. inclusive tour fares and packages also aimed at the European market have formed the basis of a violent reaction against MDC now that it has become clear that a potential for Laker survival has been developed by the financial agreement.

The airlines had not pulled their punches. In particular Adam Thomson, chairman of British Caledonian, was almost 'incoherent with anger', as Kraemer later reported, at the thought that MDC should be rescuing Laker from his own failure by taking an equity stake in what he described as 'the most disruptive airline on the North Atlantic'. Thomson followed up this outburst with an equally fiery telex to General Electric in which he said: 'Assuming information supplied by John Gentling (of MDC) to Trevor Boud (of B.Cal) this morning re MDC's massive support and investment for Laker Airways is correct, B.Cal has no further interest in McDonnell Douglas aircraft.'

THE FINAL DAYS

In the face of this kind of pressure the Americans had no option but to retreat. The first to back down was General Electric. 'There's no way that we are putting equity into Laker,' said Brian Rowe, the head of the engine division. And the PR men were ordered to try and repair the damage. Much of the afternoon of February 2 was spent in an attempt to draft a suitably soothing press release. The object was to distance GE from Laker as far as it decently could. Eventually, after much argument, it was agreed that the best line would be that GE was going to do no more than make a short-term loan guarantee and that no direct injection of cash or equity was contemplated. Identical letters to that effect, signed by Neil Burgess, one of the company's senior US executives, were sent to all the protesting airlines. 'I hope that this will ease your mind relative to the type and extent of our participation in the Laker Airways matter,' Burgess concluded.

With this decision the rescue package, Laker's last hope, effectively fell apart. True, McDonnell Douglas's £4 million offer remained on the table but the actual cash never materialised, much to the distress of Dennis Kitching, the general manager of the Midland. Up until now Kitching had done his best to be helpful. It was only with the Midland's help that Laker had met the January 15 deadline for the repayment of some of the interest on the Airbus loan. And the bank had only increased its overdraft which now stood at some £13 million on the assumption that the American money would be forthcoming. So when, on his return in late January from a trip to Egypt, Kitching discovered that the Americans still had not paid up, he was both furious and alarmed. 'I've been diddled,' he complained. It was about this time that the bank withdrew its nominee, Bill Morrison of Thomson McLintock, from his post as Laker's finance director and replaced him with one of Britain's most eminent receivers, Bill Mackey of Ernst and Whinney.

Meanwhile Ray Colgate of the CAA had been reworking his sums in the light of Laker's latest traffic returns. The figures for the second half of January had just come in and they were so bad that Colgate concluded that his original £5 million 'headroom' figure would have to be raised to at least £10 million if the company was to pass safely through the 'March narrows'. The problem was that with GE's defection only McDonnell Douglas's £4 million was available and this, as we have already seen, was by now far from sure.

On February 2, the bankers made a last-ditch attempt to repair the damage caused by GE's decision to pull out. There was a flurry of telexes from London and the MDC headquarters in St Louis, as MDC's chief negotiator in London, John Gentling, sought approval for an MDC go-it-alone solution. This activity led to nothing except to create a shortlived atmosphere of false optimism.

One of the stranger features of the drama was the small part played by the chief actor, Freddie Laker. Figures had never been his forte: but more important, perhaps, was the fact that throughout the episode he was much preoccupied with the collapse of his third marriage to his American-born wife Patricia who had taken his four-year-old son, Freddie junior, to Florida. More than two years later I asked Laker how much he knew about what was going on at this time. 'Rather a little and it worried me a good deal,' he replied. 'The trouble was,' says Ian McIntosh of Samuel Montagu, 'that Freddie was very mercurial. He was so preoccupied with his personal problems that he never gave the thing his proper attention. At vital moments he would keep popping off to Miami to see his wife and his son.'

When Laker was told of McDonnell Douglas's last-ditch efforts, he thought he was saved when in fact the company was teetering on the verge of insolvency. On the evening of Tuesday, February 1, Laker, David Sedgewick, senior vice-president, planning, for the MDC Finance Corporation, the manager of the Clydesdale Bank and some senior members of Laker management met at a London hotel on their return from the Bank of England. As, so Laker says, both the Bank and the Midland had approved the plan, everybody was in high spirits and so the party went off to Tramps, the night club, for a sausage-and-mash victory dinner. After checking again with the Midland that all was OK, Laker said: 'All right, let's go and sell some seats.' The next day Laker took Concorde on a flight to New York where he was due to make some television advertisements. But before leaving Heathrow he was caught by a reporter from the airport news agency, Brenards. Earlier that morning he had asked Ian Wallace, the manager of the Clydesdale, if it was all right to tell the press, and on being told it was he gave his now-famous 'Flying high' interview. 'All my financial worries are over,' he declared. 'A £36 million loan has been arranged with McDonnell Douglas which, with other bits and pieces, means new investment of up to £60 million. The future of the company is now very good. In fact we are in a better position than we have ever been.'

He could not have been more wrong. On Wednesday, February 3, the day the interview was published, Colgate of the CAA phoned David Walker at the Bank of England to tell him of his conclusion that the company now probably needed an emergency transfusion of nearer £10 million than £5 million as the CAA had first thought. Kitching at the Midland was also informed and a telegram was sent to Laker in New York asking him to return straightaway so that he could be at the Midland the next morning. No reason, however, was given.

'DON'T TELL FREDDIE'

That evening Ray Colgate, vice-chairman of the CAA, invited the principal participants to dinner. Among the guests was David Sedgewick of MDC. He later noted in his diary that the CAA was now insisting that the backers should give 'an unlimited guarantee' that they would prop Laker up until at least September, otherwise there was 'no chance for Freddie'. The reason why the CAA was insisting on support until September was that if Laker went bust sometime in mid-summer, when the tourist boom would be at its height, the expense of reimbursing all the passengers would wipe out the £18–£20 million in the reserve fund set up by the travel industry after the Clarkson crash in 1974. By the time the dinner party ended at midnight it was clear to everybody that there was now no hope. 'But,' Sedgewick noted, 'we agreed not to tell Freddie.' The feeling was, it appears, that to have Freddie charging about like a wounded bull would only complicate matters. Late that evening, just as he was about to step on the plane, Laker called Sedgewick from New York to ask if everything was OK. Sedgewick was less than frank. He muttered something about the CAA not being satisfied with the cash availability. But before putting the phone down, he said: 'No problems. See you tomorrow.' Later Sedgewick was to explain that he had not been able to tell Laker the truth as he had been sworn to secrecy.

The die was cast, but it was left to the Midland to take the final decision. On the morning of Thursday, February 4, Laker returned from New York and after a wash and brush-up and a change of shirt went straight to the Midland. Laker himself takes up the story. 'I was shown into a little room and then Gillespie, the deputy general manager of the Midland, came in. He shut the door and then stood with his back against it. He looks at me and says, "We want you to call in the receiver." ' Laker was stunned.

'When?' he asked.

'Now,' Gillespie replied.

'What happens if I don't?' Laker inquired.

'If you don't, we will,' Gillespie said.

Laker then turned to David Sedgewick of MDC and asked: 'Did you know this when I spoke to you last night?'

'Yes,' Sedgewick answered.

'Then why didn't you tell me?' Laker inquired.

'I was sworn to secrecy.'

By this time the room had become quite crowded and to each new arrival Laker put the same question. 'Why was I not told?' And in each case the answer was the same: 'We agreed not to tell you, Freddie.' At this point, Laker says, 'I began to feel a bit lonely.' He was told that unless he could find the necessary cash by Friday morning, the Midland would have to call in the receiver.

Laker spent that afternoon on the phone. Among the people he called was Ian Sproat who as junior minister in charge of aviation policy had, as we have seen, approved the Pan Am price cuts which had so grievously damaged Laker. Through this channel a message was sent to the Prime Minister, Margaret Thatcher, who at the Tory Party conference earlier in the year had said: 'Competition works! It is thanks to Freddie Laker that you can cross the Atlantic for so much less than it would have cost in the early 1970s.' In Whitehall Freddie was known as the

Prime Minister's 'Knight in a shining fuselage'. There was also a personal connection. Mrs Thatcher's husband Denis and Sir Freddie were at one time both members of the board of Castrol, the motor oil company, later bought by Burmah Oil. But although there was plenty of sympathy, the Government could think of no way in which it could help even though it had played an important part in the fateful Airbus deal.

In desperation Laker threw himself on the mercy of one of his competitors, Harry Goodman of Intasun, the tour operators. A midnight meeting was arranged at the Gatwick Hilton at which Laker asked Goodman if he would put up the cash in return for either one of the Airbuses or the two of Laker's profitable travel companies. But Goodman was not interested: he had been too badly burned by Laker in the past to help him out now. Laker spent much of the night on the phone to Japan in an attempt to persuade Mitsui to help out. But to no avail. And so at a meeting of the Laker Airways board at Gatwick at 8 am, the decision was taken to call in the receiver. The long battle was over.

Within the trade Bill Mackey, the receiver, has long had a reputation as a tough and very competent operator. About a week before the final collapse on Friday, February 5, Mackey had been put into Laker Airways by a now despairing Midland Bank as an 'adviser', replacing his fellow accountant Bill Morrison of Thompson McClintock who had been acting throughout the crisis as an ad hoc finance director. Though unannounced, Mackey's appointment was the first clear indication that the bank was about to pull the plug on Laker. In great secrecy Mackey assembled a ten-man team of what he calls his 'gunmen' under the code-name Operation Crash Landing. The night before the crash Mackey had sent his right-hand man, Nigel Hamilton, down to Gatwick airport where Laker had its headquarters. And by the time Mackey and his 'gunmen' arrived, Hamilton was already in the Gatwick control tower ordering the Laker planes to return to base immediately. Freddie Laker was no longer in charge: the pilots, just like everybody else, had to take their orders from the receiver. On Hamilton's instructions one plane was turned round in the air while the remainder hurried back to Gatwick. 'We had to act fast and decisively,' said Mackey. 'If just one of those planes had landed at a foreign airport and had been seized by the creditors, who knows when we would have got it back?' It was a job that took most of the first day.

But it was not the only worry. Besides the planes, there were some 8000 stranded passengers, many of whom had paid for their return tickets and had somehow to be brought back to England. But how was it to be done and who was to pay for it? Mackey saw no reason why he should. To try and solve this problem Mackey summoned a meeting of all airlines operating across the Atlantic. 'It was,' Mackey recalls, 'a very "strong" meeting. We discussed the responsibility of the airlines to clean up their own vomit. I told them: "You helped create this dog's breakfast, so you can jolly well help clean it up." ' After much argument the airlines finally agreed to bring back the stranded Laker passengers on a stand-by basis and that if they turned up within a month they could travel free or at least not be charged extra.

Mackey then turned his attention to what was his main business: the sale of the fast-dwindling Laker empire. The planes could wait. 'I was bombarded with people who wanted to buy an aircraft for fourpence,' Mackey says. The ten McDonnell Douglas DC10s stayed at Gatwick for some weeks before being flown off to the Arizona Desert and mothballed while two of the three Airbus Industrie A300 Airbuses, the pride of the Laker fleet, were eventually sold to Air Jamaica for $42 million.

The most urgent problem was the disposal of Laker's two travel companies, Arrowsmith and Laker Air Travel, which Mackey described as a 'melting ice-cream . . . Once the company had gone bust, the value of these businesses was going down day by day,' Mackey says. 'If we had waited too long there would have been nothing to sell.' Laker crashed on a Friday, but despite the weekend Mackey was in no mind to hang about. Potential buyers were told that the offer documents would be available the following Tuesday evening and that they had just twenty-four hours in which to make their bids. After some haggling and one all-night session Arrowsmith went to Greenall Whitley, the brewers, for £4 million, while Laker Air Travel was sold to Saga Holidays for £500,000.

Of the author of all this activity, Sir Freddie Laker himself, there was no sign: he spent the days immediately after the crash at the offices of Lonrho, the international trading group, trying with the help of Lonrho's mercurial founder, Tiny Rowland, to get his so-called People's Airline off the ground. In the days that followed there were a number of contacts between the two camps as Lonrho accountants tried to argue that the project was a viable proposition, but the hard-headed Mackey was not impressed. 'You can't start an airline with no planes and no licence,' he said. His scepticism proved justified when six weeks later the Civil Aviation Authority refused the People's Airline a licence. In reality it was doomed from the start.

However traumatic Sir Freddie may have found the experience his relations with Mackey himself remained surprisingly good. After it was all over Mackey invited Sir Freddie to dinner, which prompted Laker to remark that this must be the first time the victim had dined with his executioner after the event.

Two and a half years later I went to see Laker at the office of Skytrain Holidays, the cut-price travel company he had set up after the crash with the backing of Tiny Rowland's Lonrho. Apart from Sir Freddie and myself, the office on the third floor of an anonymous block in the unprepossessing surroundings of Purley, Surrey, was deserted. The only visitor that morning was a man from British Telecom who had called to take the telephones away.

On the walls there still hung mementos of former glories: there were honorary degrees from universities awarded for Sir Freddie's 'achievements in the field of civil aviation' and in pride of place was a portrait of Sir Freddie himself against a patriotic and aeronautical background. In paint at least, the popular image of Sir Freddie as the swashbuckling, flag-waving entrepreneur lived on.

But the business had not been a success. The last thing his rivals had wanted was to see Laker back in the travel business and his application to join ABTA, the Association of British

Travel Agents, had been rejected. Without ABTA's approval the business stood little chance. But Sir Freddie fights on, seemingly undismayed.

Only a small percentage of the £260 million that Laker Airways owed when it went down has yet been recovered. As nearly all the aircraft have now been sold the banks have got at least some of their money back. It is thought that Mitsui, who took back their DC10s, even made a handsome profit. But McDonnell Douglas and GE have taken big losses, as have those 17,500 Laker passengers who bought scheduled Skytrain tickets at a cost of £4 million and were therefore not covered by the travel industry's insurance scheme. Immediately after the crash Tiny Rowland offered to reimburse these passengers, but when the Lonrho/Laker People's Airline failed to get off the ground this gesture somehow never materialised.

At the end of 1982 the Laker liquidator, Christopher Morris of Touche Ross, calculated that the unsecured creditors, including some of Laker's own employees, were still owed about £14.7 million. In an attempt to recover this money Morris has launched a series of legal actions in both America and the UK alleging that Laker has been the victim of a conspiracy by the international airlines who fixed prices and wrecked the McDonnell Douglas rescue package in order to drive him out of business. As we have seen there is clearly something in Morris's claim. Nobody can deny that Pan Am's decision in November 1981 to match Laker's fares on the North Atlantic had a catastrophic effect on Laker's business. But whether or not Pan Am and the others actually conspired together illegally to fix prices is arguable. In December 1984 President Reagan ordered the anti-trust division of the US Justice Department to drop its investigation. But at the time of writing, the business of the 'nastygrams' and the undoubted pressure brought by the airlines on McDonnell Douglas and General Electric to abandon their rescue efforts has yet to be tested in the courts.

Laker himself, however, has emerged in comparatively good shape. The blow has been more to his pride than his pocket. At the time of the crash Laker had, he says, a personal overdraft of £1 million and had given personal guarantees of some £600,000.

He was, he says, forced to sell a large number of stocks and shares on which, eventually, he had to pay capital gains tax. Most of the trappings of the tycoon have been sold to meet these debts. The 584-acre stud farm at East Horsley in Surrey, the yacht, *Patricia*, and the Rolls, the last of some twenty-five which Laker has owned, have all gone. Only the much-prized personalised number plate, FLY 1, has been saved and now adorns a secondhand Volkswagen. Laker himself now drives a T-registered Jaguar. He is, however, not exactly poor. He earns a decent living as a consultant to a number of airlines and hotel companies, and retains his Tudor farmhouse and eighty acres of land at Chailey in Sussex. 'I've got to live somewhere,' he says. The crash does not seem to have dented his self-confidence: he remains as ebullient as ever. 'I could have shot myself, or taken to drink, or run away,' he says. 'But I didn't. I stayed to face the music. I may these days be more infamous than famous but nobody has ever said that I took a penny piece for myself.'

There is a curious tailpiece to the Laker story. In the dog days following the crash when all his hopes of re-establishing himself as a big operator on the international scene had faded to nothing, Sir Freddie had another idea. He launched something called the Laker Cube, something which people could play with to while away a long air journey. The toy was made up of metal cubes magnetised in such a way that there was only one combination in which they would fit together. One mistake – and the whole thing fell to pieces. A better epitaph could not have been devised.

Postscript

OVER THE PAST century there have been enormous changes in the pattern of economic life and behaviour which in turn have radically altered society's attitudes. Debt is no longer a matter of shame and embarrassment as it was in Joseph Chamberlain's day. Everybody lives on credit these days and though a bouncing cheque may be inconvenient it no longer leads to expulsion from polite society.

The Cork Committee's investigation was the work of a high-powered team of some thirty-five bankers, lawyers, academics and accountants. Its report, which ran to over a quarter of a million words, took five and a half years to prepare and led to conclusions which were radical and fundamental. The committee took as its starting point the assumption that 'the answers given by English law today . . . do not seem to us to be in tune with the modern world but to be responses to the economic problems and attitudes prevalent over 100 years ago. Despite the fundamental changes in society and in commercial life which have occurred since then, the system for dealing with problems created by insolvency has been tinkered with, patched and extended by false analogies, inconsistencies and deficiencies. They do not accomplish what is required of them; moreover, they no longer accord with what the general public conceive to be the demands of fairness and justice to all in a modern society.'

In its White Paper of February 1984 the Government acknowledged that there is 'an urgent need for reform'. But though there were a number of technical changes designed to curb some – but not all – of the specific abuses I have described in the preceding chapters, there was little attempt to tailor the structure of insolvency law and practise to meet modern conditions. Beneath the arid technicalities the assumptions that under-pinned Joseph Chamberlain's Act of 1883 remain intact.

The passage of the legislation proved to be far more controversial than anyone anticipated. The Government suffered two major defeats in the House of Lords and the career of the junior Minister responsible was blighted: he lost his job in the next reshuffle. Altogether what was intended as a modest proposal of some 200 clauses attracted nearly 1400 amendments and the hostility of the accounting profession, the CBI, the Institute of Directors and the National Consumer Council.

While this debate was still in progress, I called on Sir Kenneth Cork and asked him for his reactions to the Government's proposals. Sir Kenneth is a forthright man and characteristically he made no attempt to hide his disappointment. 'All the Government has done is to try and clear up a number of abuses. If that's all they wanted we could have done that job in a year and a half. But that was not what our report was about. I realise that it would have taken a full Parliamentary session to implement the full report. But I'm not a Parliamentarian and they should have thought about that before they asked us to do the job.'

Perhaps the biggest missed opportunity in the 1985 Insolvency Act is the Government's failure to do more than tinker with the law of limited liability. In my travels around the insolvency world, I found widespread criticism, even from the most dyed-in-the-wool practitioners who felt that the protection afforded by the law was far too wide. As Cork himself said to me: 'Limited liability is not a right but a privilege which should be taken away from those who abuse it.'

Introduced in the early 1860s to encourage risk-taking, it has become, as I showed in Chapter Seven, an umbrella under which the unscrupulous can all too easily shelter. When a company goes under the creditors, including ordinary customers, almost invariably suffer but equally the directors or owners often emerge virtually scot-free – thanks to the law of limited liability.

As a means of encouraging enterprise and protecting the unlucky or the imprudent from the full consequences of their actions, the law has proved an effective and useful instrument.

But it is also, as we have seen, open to widespread abuse. Without the protection of limited liability, the change-the-name-the-game's-the-same artists would not have flourished to anything like the same degree.

Theoretically the existing laws against fraud should have put a stop to this sort of thing. But as I have said, prosecutions are few and far between, largely because of the difficulty of proving an intent to defraud, as the law requires. In his report Cork proposed an easy remedy: anybody whose company went bust twice within five years should, he suggested, automatically lose the protection of limited liability and would thus become personally liable for the debts he had incurred. 'The object', says Cork, 'was to hit the delinquent director where it hurts most – in his pocket.'

But this remedy proved to be far too radical for a business-minded Tory government. The Government rejected Cork's proposals as being too 'far-reaching'. 'Whilst they would curb the activities of the delinquent director,' the White Paper concluded, 'they would at the same time deter the genuine entrepreneur from risking his capital in a further venture.' On the losses suffered by the creditors and the customers who may have been cheated and defrauded nothing is said.

The problem of the rogue director has not been wholly ignored. The Government has acknowledged that the ease with which an operator can close down a company only to set up another very similar enterprise the very next day is nothing short of a scandal. But the proposed remedies fall well short of Cork's robust proposals.

The Government's first rather bold idea that any director involved in a compulsory liquidation should automatically be disqualified was greeted with a chorus of protest from all sides. Invented by the civil servants at the Department of Trade and Industry who somehow failed to consult with the professionals, it was a concept doomed from the start. Not only would the directors involved in voluntary liquidations, the main problem area as we have seen, have escaped all penalty but the provision would have been counter-productive in that it was thought likely to have deterred part-time directors brought in specifically to help save companies.

In the face of these objections the Government retreated. Directors can still be disqualified but it is no longer automatic and applies only after a rather cumbersome and hitherto untested procedure involving the liquidator, the receiver, the Secretary of State and the courts has been set in motion. If at the end of all this, the director is disqualified, he becomes personally liable for the company's debts. The effect could be similar to the one Kenneth Cork was trying to achieve but the route is roundabout and the outcome uncertain.

Disqualification is one of the Government's new weapons; the threat of a prosecution by the courts for what is described as 'wrongful trading' is another. In future any director who allows his company to continue trading after it has become clear that it is insolvent can be prosecuted and the director concerned will, on conviction, lose the protection of limited liability. This is a new concept which if rigorously enforced could, so Sir Kenneth believes, have some effect. 'It is not as effective as our own proposals', he says. 'But it might do the trick.'

Whether it does or not will partly depend on the attitude of the courts but even more on the willingness of creditors to bring such actions. The great weakness of all legislation in this field, so the professionals say, is that those who have been cheated, defrauded or otherwise lost out have to finance the costs of any legal action out of their own pockets. This is something that no matter how aggrieved they may be, they are normally understandably reluctant to do: having lost out in a company crash, the idea of throwing good money after bad in an attempt to recoup their losses and to bring the architects of the disaster to book is often not very appealing. It was for this reason that Cork suggested that in any crash 10 per cent of the assets should be held back on behalf of the unsecured creditors. This idea was flatly rejected by the Government on the grounds that the monies realised would in the vast majority of cases be so small as to make little or no difference. Here again, Cork argues, the Government has misunderstood what he was driving at. 'What they have failed to grasp', he says, 'is that the money was not intended to pay off the unsecured creditors but to give the liquidator some funds so that he can fight for their interests.

Without any cash, he is powerless.'

The commonest complaint of honest company directors who have been through the insolvency mill is about the practitioners of the private sector. It is felt that though they may do a good job for the bank which has appointed them, in the rush to realise the assets, the wider interests of the company, the shareholders and last but not least the employees are often ignored as we saw in the sad case of Stone-Platt. Nearly every director I talked to complained of assets being sold off too quickly and too cheaply, and of profitable subsidiaries being dragged down with the main company. Receivers were regarded as being too tough, too arrogant and accountable only to their paymasters, the banks. Frequently it was suggested to me that the American so-called Chapter Eleven system under which the insolvent company passes into the care of a court-supervised committee consisting both of outsiders and the old management with a view to salvaging as much as possible from the wreckage was a fairer, more humane and more efficient way of dealing with the problem. From the day of the crash Leslie Pincott of Stone-Platt has argued that this would have been the best solution for his stricken company.

In trying to reform the system, the Government has borrowed something from the Americans. The act introduces the administrator, a figure new to the insolvency scene in that, unlike the receiver, he is responsible not to the banks but to the court which appoints him. But at the same time the managers of an insolvent company, unlike in America, will not be allowed much of a look-in.

Britain's insolvency practitioners whose vested interest in the present set-up is both strong and self-evident are quick to defend the status quo. 'Why on earth should one hand back the management to the very people who caused the trouble in the first place?', asks Sir Kenneth Cork. It is a powerful argument; and there is little academic research to demonstrate that the American system is inherently better than our own. And yet those who complain that the insolvency practitioners have too much power have a very real point. The majority are probably honest and well-meaning. But there is plenty of scope, as we

187

have seen in Chapter Six, for rogues. And yet the mechanism for calling receivers and liquidators to account is weak and ineffective. Committees of inspection are ignored; company law is manipulated in order to override or to disregard the interests of creditors and customers; and no one, at the end of the day, bothers to check exactly what a receiver or a liquidator has been up to. This is not just an debating point: in the course of their work receivers and liquidators often handle very large sums of money – millions of pounds in some cases. And yet there is no requirement that their figures should be independently audited. True, the final accounts of a receivership do have to be presented to the Department of Trade but its harrassed officials are usually far too busy to conduct a proper check. It is a legal requirement that a company's books should be audited by a professional outsider: it is time the accountants themselves were subjected to the same discipline.

If the track record of the insolvency practitioners was spotless these points would have less force. But it is not. Over the years those involved in the insolvency business, the accountants, the solicitors, the valuers and the estate agents, have demonstrated time and again that they can be just as greedy, incompetent, and sometimes dishonest as other folk. The professionals argue that the black sheep are only a tiny minority but that doesn't weaken the argument for proper supervision and adequate control.

The Government has attempted to put a stop to some of the most notorious abuses. In addition to the 'wrongful trading' proposals already described, some of the cowboys' favourite tricks have been proscribed. There are provisions in the act designed to end the manipulation of company meetings to the advantage of the directors and to the detriment of creditors; the powers of the provisional liquidators who jump in to loot a company of its assets before anybody realises what is going on have been curtailed.

The Government has also tried to tackle head on the problem of the cowboys – but with only limited success. In its original form the White Paper laid down that only properly qualified persons such as accountants and solicitors should be allowed to practise with special transitional arrangements for unqualified but experienced members of the Insolvency Practitioners Association. But faced with opposition from inside the profession, this measure has been watered down to the point where Sir Kenneth Cork believes it will be ineffectual. 'It's the old story', he says. 'There is always pressure from those who are running a business to be allowed to continue as before.'

The bulk of the act's provisions deal with the corporate sector. But of the plight of the ordinary bankrupt which I described in the opening chapters, the act says remarkably little.

The most important change is that there is now greater scope for a small debtor to come to an arrangement with his creditors without being sucked into the great bankruptcy machine. The process of going bankrupt is to be streamlined and simplified. From now on the Official Receiver will normally no longer play a part in cases involving less than £15,000 and the threshold below which it is impossible to go bust will be lifted from £200 to £750 to take account of inflation. But as the lawyers and the accountants will still take their cut just as before, the cost of bankruptcy seems likely to remain as high as ever. Nor have any of the anachronistic civil disabilities been removed. Attitudes to divorce, illegitimacy, homosexuality and other forms of sexual and other behaviour have changed out of all recognition over the past generation or so. But society, it seems, is as determined as ever to punish with undue severity those whose only offence is that they owe money they are unable to repay. It is often argued that innocent creditors invariably suffer also with much less reason. Quite so: but that is no reason to hammer the bankrupt into the ground.

APPENDIX ONE

A short guide to Barry Freeman's businesses

Pre-1980 Usoworth Ltd – failed
1980   Henley Properties Ltd – compulsory liquidation, October 13, 1980
           Jobed Ltd – incorporated August 7, 1980 – trading as Cash Flow Investment Services (CFIS)
           Stargrange Ltd – trading as CFIS
           Cash Flow Investment Services (CFIS) – business name registered November 1, 1980
1981   BB Commercial Enterprises – business name registered July 1981
           BBCE moves into Stargrange offices. Stargrange left in limbo
           Jobed Ltd – creditors' meeting called December 14, 1981
1982   Formation of Photo-Fast (UK) Ltd; Gilmartin Property Co Ltd; BB Commercial Enterprises Ltd, February 11, 1982
1983   Jobed Ltd – compulsorily wound up February 7. Official Receiver appointed provisional liquidator

APPENDIX TWO

A short guide to Sydney Newman's businesses

1969   Loft Rooms (Ilford) Ltd – wound up
        Loft Rooms (London) Ltd – wound up

1970
1971 } Various dishwasher sales companies formed
1972

1973   Dishmaster Ltd – voluntary liquidation
        Bridgedec Ltd – compulsory liquidation
        Lylybet Dishwashers (UK) Ltd formed

1977   Lylybet Dishwashers (North West) Ltd – compulsory
        liquidation

1978   Lylybet Dishwashers (East Midlands) Ltd – dissolved
        Loft Rooms (Southern) Ltd – formed
        Loft Rooms (London) Ltd – ceases trading
        Lylybet Dishwashers (Southern) Ltd – declared insol-
        vent
        Loft Rooms (Southern) Ltd – name changed to Loft
        Rooms Ltd

1980   Lylybet Dishwashers (UK) Ltd – voluntary liquida-
        tion
        Dishmaster (Home Counties) Ltd takes over spares
        manufacture
        Dishmaster (Home Counties) Ltd changes name to
        Dishmaster (Lylybet) Ltd

Index